The Inns and Taverns of "Pickwick"

Bertram Waldrom Matz

Copyright Notice

The text in this book has been downloaded from the internet and has been extensively edited and typeset.

Copyright © 2006 Objective Systems Pty Ltd ACN 085 119 953

TABLE OF CONTENTS

Chapter I	1
Chapter II	9
Chapter III	17
Chapter IV	27
Chapter V	35
Chapter VI	45
Chapter VII	55
Chapter VIII	63
Chapter IX	71
Chapter X	79
Chapter XI	87
Chapter XII	99
Chapter XIII	107
Chapter XIV	115
Chapter XV	123
Chapter XVI	133
Chapter XVII	139
Chapter XVIII	149

The Inns and Taverns of "Pickwick"
With Some Observations on their Other Associations

Chapter I

"PICKWICK" AND THE COACHING AGE
***

Dickens, like all great authors, had a tendency to underestimate the value of his most popular book. At any rate, it is certainly on record that he thought considerably more of some of his other works than he did of the immortal Pickwick. But The Pickwick Papers has maintained its place through generations, and retains it to-day, as the most popular book in our language – a book unexampled in our literature. There are persons who make a yearly custom of reading it; others who can roll off pages of it from memory; scores who can answer any meticulous question in an examination of its contents; and a whole army ready and waiting to correct any misquotation that may appear in print from its pages. All its curiosities, lapses, oddities, anachronisms, slips and misprints have been discovered by commentators galore, and the number of books it has brought into existence is stupendous.

What the secret of its popularity is would take a volume to make manifest; but in a word, one might attribute it to its vividness of reality – to the fact that every character seems to be a real living being, with whose minute peculiarities we are made familiar in a singularly droll and happy manner. With each we become close friends on first acquaintance, and as episode succeeds episode the friendship deepens, with no thought that our friends are mere imaginary creatures of the author's brain.

It does not matter if the adventures of these amiable and jovial beings are boisterously reckless at times, or if they indulge in impossible probabilities. Their high spirited gaiety and inexhaustible fun and humour and their overflow of good-nature stifles criticism.

Dickens's object in writing The Pickwick Papers he assured us in the preface was "to place before the reader a constant succession of characters and incidents; to paint them in as vivid colours as he could command, and to render them, at the same time, life-like and amusing." All this he succeeded in doing with such amazing success that we have a masterly picture of English life of the period to be found in no other book. The secret of the book's popularity and fame is in its unaffected and flowing style, its dramatic power, and, of course, its exuberant humour.

But there is much for serious reflection in its pages as well, and one could dilate at length on the propaganda which is so thinly camouflaged throughout; propaganda against lawyers, prisons, corruption in Parliament, celebrity hunting, pomposity, fraud, hypocrisy and all uncharitableness in the abstract; but all this is wrapped up in the same way that such things are done in all the fairy tales of which Pickwick is one of the best.

There are, as a fact, innumerable reasons why Pickwick is so popular, so necessary to-day. The one which concerns us more at the moment is its appeal as a mirror of the manners and customs of a romantic age which has fast receded from us. It is, perhaps, the most accurate picture extant of the old coaching era and all that was corollary to it. No writer has done more than Dickens to reflect the glory of that era, and the glamour and comfort of the old inns of England which in those days were the havens of the road to every traveller. All his books abound in pleasant and faithful pictures of the times, and alluring and enticing descriptions of those old hostelries where not only ease was sought and expected, but obtained; Pickwick is packed with them.

The outside appearance of an inn alone was in those times so well considered that it addressed a cheerful front towards the traveller "as a home of entertainment ought, and tempted him with many mute but significant assurances of a comfortable welcome." Its very signboard promised good cheer and meant it; the attractive furnishing of the homely windows, the bright flowers on the sills seemed to beckon one to "come in"; and when one did enter, one was greeted and cared for as a guest and not merely as a customer.

We all know, as Dickens has reminded us elsewhere, the great station hotel, belonging to the company of proprietors which has suddenly sprung up in any place we like to name, ". . . in which we can get anything we want, after its kind, for money; but where nobody is glad to see us, or sorry to see us, or minds (our bill paid) whether we come or go, or how, or when, or why, or cares about us . . . where we have no individuality, but put ourselves into the general post, as it were, and are sorted and disposed of according to our division." That is more the modern method and is in direct contrast to the old coaching method, which, alas! may never return, of which the inns in Pickwick furnish us with glowing examples.

We certainly are coming back to these roadside inns in the present age of rapid motor transit; yet we are in too much of a tearing hurry to make the same use of the old inns as they did in the more leisurely age.

We believe these old inns attract to-day not only because of their quaintness and the old-world atmosphere which adheres to them, but because of the tradition which clings to them; and the most popular tradition of all, and the one of which the proprietors are most proud, is the Dickens tradition.

There are scores of such inns in the city of London and throughout the country whose very names immediately conjure up some merry scene in his books and revive never-to-be-forgotten memories of exhilarating incidents.

Time, the devastating builder, and the avaricious landlord have played havoc with many. Several, however, remain to tell their own tale, whilst the memory of others is sustained by a modern building bearing the old name, all of which are landmarks for the Dickens lover.

Many of them, of course, existed only in the novelist's fertile imagination; but most of them had foundation in reality, and most of them, particularly in Pickwick, are mentioned by name and have become immortal in consequence; and were it not for the popularity of his writings, their fame in many instances would have deserted them and their glory have departed.

Inns, hotels and wayside public-houses play a most important part in The Pickwick Papers, and many of the chief scenes are enacted within their walls. The book, indeed, opens in an hotel and ends in one. The first scene arising from the projected "journeys and investigations" of those four distinguished members of the Club took place in an hotel, or – to speak correctly – outside one, namely, the "Golden Cross" at Charing Cross. There is even an earlier reference to a public-house near St. Martin's le Grand, from where the "first cab was fetched," whilst the last important incident of the book was enacted in another, the Adelphi Hotel off the Strand, when Mr. Pickwick announced his determination to retire into private life at Dulwich.

In the ensuing pages, the Pickwickians are followed in the tours they made in pursuit of adventure, and the inns and taverns they stopped at are taken in the order of their going and coming. With each is recalled the story, adventure, or scene associated with it, and if it has any history of its own apart from that gained through the book, record is made of the facts concerning it.

The Pickwick Papers was completed in 1837, and a dinner was given to celebrate the event, at which Dickens himself presided and his friend, Serjeant T. N. Talfourd, to whom the book was dedicated, acted as vice-chairman. Ainsworth, Forster, Lover, Macready, Jerdan and other close friends were invited, and the dinner took place at The Prince of Wales Coffee House and Hotel in Leicester Place, Leicester Square.

It is very curious that no extended account of this historic event exists. Forster, in his biography of the novelist, beyond saying that "everybody in hearty good-humour with every other body," and that "our friend Ainsworth was of the company," is otherwise silent over the event. There is certainly a reference to the dinner in a letter from Dickens to Macready, dated from "48 Doughty Street, Wednesday Evening," with no date to it, in which he says:

> "There is a semi-business, semi-pleasure little dinner which I intend to give at the 'Prince of Wales,' in Leicester Place, Leicester Square, on Saturday, at five for half-past precisely, at which Talfourd, Forster, Ainsworth, Jerdan, and the publishers will be present. It is to celebrate (that is too great a word, but I can think of no better) the conclusion of my Pickwick labours; and so I intend, before you take that roll upon the grass you spoke of, to beg your acceptance of one of the first complete copies of the work. I shall be much delighted if you will join us."

We have seen a similarly worded letter written to Samuel Lover, and no doubt each guest received such an invitation from the novelist.

The only real account of the function is contained in a letter from Ainsworth to his friend, James Crossley, which is as follows:

> "On Saturday last we celebrated the completion of The Pickwick Papers. We had a capital dinner, with capital wine and capital speeches. Dickens, of course, was in the chair. Talfourd was the Vice,

and an excellent Vice he made. . . . Just before he was about to propose THE toast of the evening the headwaiter – for it was at a tavern that the carouse took place – entered, and placed a glittering temple of confectionery on the table, beneath the canopy of which stood a little figure of the illustrious Mr. Pickwick. This was the work of the landlord. As you may suppose, it was received with great applause. Dickens made a feeling speech in reply to the Serjeant's eulogy. . . . Just before dinner Dickens received a cheque for L750 from his publishers."

Although this hotel cannot rightly be termed a Pickwick inn in the same sense that the others in this book can, it certainly has a claim to honourable mention.

In 1823 the building in which this notable historic dinner took place was known as The Prince of Wales Coffee House and Hotel. When it ceased to be an hotel we are unable to state, but in 1890 it was a French Hospital and Dispensary, ten years later it was let out as offices, and in 1913 it was a foreign club; but the building is practically the same as it was in 1837.

Chapter II

THE "GOLDEN CROSS," CHARING CROSS
***

Before the "Golden Cross" was given such prominence in The Pickwick Papers, it formed the subject of one of the chapters in Dickens's previous book, Sketches by Boz. But although there is a "Golden Cross" still standing at Charing Cross to-day, and a fairly old inn to boot, it is not the actual one which figures in these two books and in David Copperfield.

As a matter of fact, there have been several "Golden Crosses" at Charing Cross; one, perhaps the first, stood in the village of Charing in 1643. But the one which claims our attention stood on the exact spot where now towers the Nelson Monument in Trafalgar Square, and was the busiest coaching inn in the west end of London. In front of it was the King Charles statue and the ancient cross of Charing. Close at hand was Northumberland House with its famous lion overlooking the scene.

This "Golden Cross" was either rebuilt in 1811 or in that year had its front altered to the Gothic style. Whichever is the case, it was this Gothic inn that Dickens knew and described in his books. It was demolished in 1827, or thereabouts, to make room for the improvements in the neighbourhood which developed, into the Trafalgar Square we all know to-day. It was then that the present building, facing Charing Cross Station, was erected, which, also in its turn, has had a new frontage.

Dickens in his early youth, whilst employed in a blacking warehouse at Hungerford Stairs and during his youthful wanderings, became intimately acquainted with the district. When, therefore, in the early 'thirties he commenced his literary career, he recalled those early days and placed on permanent record his impressions of what he then saw, amongst which was the Golden Cross Hotel.

And so we find that in writing the chapter in Sketches by Boz on "Early Coaches" he chooses the "Golden Cross" of his boyhood for its chief incident, an incident which no doubt happened to himself in his early manhood. He had risen early on a certain cold morning to catch the early coach to Birmingham – perhaps to fulfil one of his reporting engagements:

"It strikes 5:15," he says, "as you trudge down Waterloo Place on your way to the 'Golden Cross,' and you discover for the first time that you were called an hour too early. You have no time to go back, and there is no place open to go into, and you have therefore no recourse but to go forward. You arrive at the office. . . . You wander into the booking office.

. . . There stands the identical book-keeper in the same position, as if he had not moved since you saw him yesterday. He informs you that the coach is up the yard, and will be brought round in about 15 minutes. . . . You retire to the tap-room . . . for the purpose of procuring some hot brandy and water, which you do – when the kettle boils, an event which occurs exactly two and a half minutes before the time fixed for the starting of the coach. The first stroke of six peals from St. Martin's Church steeple as you take the first sip of the boiling liquid. You find yourself in the booking office in two seconds, and the tap waiter finds himself much comforted by your brandy and water in about the same period. . . . The horses are in. . . . The place which a few minutes ago was so still and quiet is all bustle. 'All right,' sings the guard . . . and off we start as briskly as if the morning were all right as well as the coach."

One of Cruikshank's pictures illustrates the above scene in the booking office, and in it one of the figures represents Dickens himself as he appeared at the period. Dotted about on the walls are bills in which the name of the hotel is very conspicuous.

In chapter two of The Pickwick Papers we get a further glimpse of the inn, centring in a more exhilarating and epoch-making incident. The Pickwickians were to start on their memorable peregrinations from the "Golden Cross" for Rochester by the famous "Commodore" coach; and Mr. Pickwick having hired a cabriolet in the neighbourhood of his lodgings in Goswell Street arrived at the hotel in order to meet his friends for the purpose. On alighting, and having tendered his fare, an animated incident with the cabman, who accused him of being an informer, ensued, and ended in the assault and battery described in the following words:

"The cabman dashed his hat upon the ground with a reckless disregard of his own private property, and knocked Mr. Pickwick's spectacles off, and followed up the attack with a blow on Mr. Pickwick's nose and another on Mr. Pickwick's chest; and a third in Mr. Snodgrass's eye; and a fourth, by way of variety, in Mr. Tupman's waistcoat, and then danced into the road and then back again to the pavement, and finally dashed the whole temporary supply of breath out of Mr. Winkle's body; and all in half a dozen seconds."

The embarrassing situation was only saved by the intervention of Mr. Jingle, who quickly settled the cabman and escorted Mr. Pickwick into the travellers' waiting-room and had a raw beefsteak applied to Mr. Pickwick's eye, which had been badly mauled by the irate cabman. All things righted themselves, however, and the merry party left the "Golden Cross" on the coach for their journey to Rochester, to the accompaniment of Mr. Jingle's staccato tones as they drove through the archway, warning the company to take care of their heads:

"'Terrible place – dangerous work – other day – five children – mother – tall lady, eating sandwiches-forgot the arch – crash – knock – children look round – mother's head off – sandwich in her hand – no mouth to put it in – head of family off – shocking – shocking.'"

The arch referred to by our jesting friend can be seen in the picture here shown.

The "Golden Cross" also figures prominently in David Copperfield on the occasion of the arrival of the hero of the book from Canterbury:

"We went to the 'Golden Cross,'" he says, "then a mouldy sort of establishment in a close neighbourhood. A waiter showed me into the coffee-room, and a chambermaid introduced me to my small bedchamber, which smelt like a hackney coach and was shut up like a family vault."

Later in the evening he met his old school friend, Steerforth, who was evidently on better and more familiar terms with the waiter, for he not only demanded, but secured a better bedroom for David.

"I found my new room a great improvement on my old one," he says, "it not being at all musty and having a fourpost bedstead in it, which was quite a little landed estate. Here, among pillows enough for six, I soon fell asleep in a blissful condition, and dreamed of ancient Rome, Steerforth and friendship, until the early morning coaches rumbling out of the archway underneath made me dream of thunder and the gods."

This comfortable new aspect of the inn did not stop at his bedroom, for he took breakfast the next morning "in a snug private apartment, red-curtained and Turkey carpeted, where the fire burnt bright and a fine hot breakfast was set forth on a table covered with a clean cloth. . . . I could not enough admire the change Steerforth had wrought in the 'Golden Cross'; or compose the dull, forlorn state I had held yesterday with this morning's comfort and this morning's entertainment."

It was on another occasion later in the story that David Copperfield, then lodging in Buckingham Street close by, encountered poor old Peggotty on the steps of St. Martin's Church. It was a snowy, dismal night and Peggotty was resting on his journey in search for Little Emily.

"In those days," says Dickens, "there was a side entrance to the stable yard of the 'Golden Cross' nearly opposite to where we stood. I pointed out the gateway, put my arm through his, and we went across. Two or three public rooms opened out of the stable yard; and looking into one of them, and finding it empty, and a good fire burning, I took him in there."

The side entrance here referred to was at the time in St. Martin's Lane – that part of it which then ran down from St. Martin's Church to the Strand. It led into the stable yard, backing into what is now Trafalgar Square, and was part of the old inn of Pickwick and The Sketches, and not of the present one, which many topographers have asserted.

But the "Golden Cross" had its fame apart from Dickens, although it is Dickens who has immortalized its name for the general public.

As we have pointed out it was the most popular of the West End coaching inns of London. This remark applies to the various houses which have borne its name. It is recorded that as far back as 1757 coaches plied between Brighton, or Brighthelmstone as it was then called, and the "Golden Cross." The fare was 13s. – (children in lap and outside passengers half price). For years afterwards it was the favourite starting-place for the famous Brighton coaches, and in 1821 forty were running to and fro daily.

Coaches from the same inn served Exeter, Salisbury, Blandford, Dorchester and Bridport; Hastings and Tunbridge Wells; Cambridge, Cheltenham, Dover, Norwich and Portsmouth. It was from here that the historic "Comet" and "Regent" to Brighton and the "Tally Ho" for Birmingham set. out on their journeys, and although the "Golden Cross" which stands to-day cannot boast the glory of the old days of the coaching era, it is still a busy centre, situated as it is in the very heart of London opposite one of its busiest railway termini.

To-day new Dickensian associations circle round it, for on certain days during the summer months motor coaches, chartered by the Dickens Fellowship, make this the starting point for their pilgrimages into Dickens-land, often taking the route the Pickwickians did, as recorded in their chronicles.

Chapter III

THE "BULL," ROCHESTER, "WRIGHT'S NEXT HOUSE" AND THE "BLUE LION," MUGGLETON
***

To the accompaniment of the "stranger's" breathless eloquence, the Pickwickians' first journey from London passed with no untoward adventure. Although the "Commodore" coach stopped occasionally to change horses and incidentally to refresh the passengers, no mention of an inn by name or any other designation is made, however, until The Bull Inn in the High Street, Rochester, is reached.

"Do you remain here, sir?" enquired Nathaniel Winkle of the "stranger."

"Here – not I – but you'd better – good house – nice beds – Wright's next house, dear – very dear – half a crown in the bill if you look at the waiter – charge you more if you dine at a friend's than they would if you dined in the coffee room – rum fellows – very."

After consultation with his friends Mr. Pickwick invited the "stranger" to dine with them, which he accepted with alacrity.

"Great pleasure – not presume to dictate, but boiled fowl and mushrooms – capital thing! What time?"

The hour being arranged they parted for the time being.

Dickens knew his Rochester well, even in the days when he was writing Pickwick – a knowledge gained doubtless when a lad at Chatham, and Jingle's reference to "Wright's next house" is evidence of this, for there was such an hotel at the time, the owner's name of which was Wright. It was a few doors away, but was actually the next public-house, which, of course, was what was meant.

Its original name was the "Crown," but in 1836 the said Wright, on becoming proprietor, altered the name it then bore to that of his own. He also changed its appearance to suit his own fancies. In the earlier days it was a typical coaching inn, and had the reputation of once having been favoured with a visit of Queen Elizabeth, as well of Hogarth and his friends. It claimed to have been built in 1390, and was then owned by Simon Potyn, who was several times member of Parliament for the city.

In an old engraving of Rochester Bridge the inn can be seen with the word "Wright's" distinctly showing in prominent letters emblazoned on its frontage, if such proof that Jingle was not romancing were necessary.

The inn was rebuilt in 1864, and has been identified as the "Crozier" of Edwin Drood, where Datchery, on his first arrival in the town "announced himself . . . as an idle dog living on his means . . . as he stood with his back to the empty fire-place, waiting for his fried sole, veal cutlet and pint of sherry."

In the meantime Mr. Pickwick and his friends, after having engaged and inspected a private sitting-room and bedrooms and ordered their dinner at "The Bull," set out to inspect the city and adjoining neighbourhood.

Before the days of Pickwick, the "Bull" presumably was merely a comfortable roadside coaching inn between Dover and London, with no claim to fame other than that of being a favoured resort of the military from the adjacent town of Chatham. It is true that Queen Victoria – then but a Princess – was compelled, because of a mishap to the bridge across the Medway and the stormy weather, to stay in the inn with her mother, the Duchess of Kent, for one night only. They were on their way to London from Dover. The event happened on the 29th of November, 1836, and caused a flutter of excitement in the city and inspired the proprietor to add the words "Royal Victoria" to the inn's name, and to justify the adornment of the front of the building with the royal crest of arms.

But it remained for the Pickwickians to draw the inn out from the ruck of the commonplace, and to spread its fame to all corners of the globe; and the fact that it once had royal patronage is nothing in comparison to the other fact that it was the headquarters of the Pickwickians on a certain memorable occasion. That is the attraction to it; that is the immutable thing that makes its name a household word wherever the English language is spoken. Indeed, that was the one notable event in its history which filled the proprietor with pride, and in his wisdom, in order to lure visitors into its comfortable interior, he could find no more magnetic announcement for the signboard on each side of the entrance than the plain unvarnished statement:

"Good House. Nice Beds. Vide Pickwick."

It may have boasted a history before then; it is difficult to say. It existed in 1827 when Dickens housed the famous four within its hospitable walls; and he doubtless knew it long before then when, as a lad, he lived in Chatham; anyway, it was always a favourite of his, and furnishes the scene of many incidents in his books, in addition to the part it plays in the early portion of The Pickwick Papers; it no doubt is the original of the "Winglebury Arms" in "The Great

Winglebury Duel" in Sketches by Boz, and is certainly the "Blue Boar" of Great Expectations.

Dickens frequented it himself, and the room he occupied on those occasions is known as the Dickens room and is furnished with pieces of furniture from his residence at Gad's Hill. We know, too, that he conducted his friends over it, on those occasions when he made pilgrimages with them around the neighbourhood.

The house has been slightly altered since those days, but it practically remains the same as when Dickens deposited the Pickwickians in its courtyard that red-letter day in 1827. Its outside is dull and sombre-looking, but its interior comfort and spaciousness soon dispel any misgivings which its exterior might have created.

The entrance hall is as spacious as it was when Dickens described it, in "The Great Winglebury Duel," as ornamented with evergreen plants terminating in a perspective view of the bar, and a glass case, in which were displayed a choice variety of delicacies ready for dressing, to catch the eye of a new-comer the moment he enters, and excite his appetite to the highest possible pitch. "Opposite doors," he says, "lead to the 'coffee' and 'commercial' rooms; and a great wide rambling staircase – three stairs and a landing – four stairs and another landing – one step and another landing – and so on – conducts to galleries of bedrooms and labyrinths of sitting-rooms, denominated 'private,' where you may enjoy yourself as privately as you can in any place where some bewildered being or other walks into your room every five minutes by mistake, and then walks out again, to open all the doors along the gallery till he finds his own."

And so the visitor finds it to-day, although the interior of the coffee-room may have been denuded of its compartments which the interview between Pip and Bentley Drummie in Great Expectations suggests were there on that occasion. It was in this room that the Pickwickians breakfasted and awaited the arrival of the chaise to take them to Dingley Dell; and it was over its blinds that Mr. Pickwick surveyed the passers-by in the street, and before which the vehicle made its appearance with the very amusing result known to all readers of the book.

The commercial room is across the yard, over which on one occasion Mr. Wopsle was reciting Collin's ode to Pip in Great Expectations with such dramatic effect that the commercials objected and sent up their compliments with the remark that "it wasn't the Tumbler's Arms."

From the hall runs the staircase upon which took place the famous scene between Dr. Slammer and Jingle, illustrated so spiritedly by Phiz. Those who remember the incident – and who does not? – can visualize it all again as they mount the stairs to the bedrooms above, which the Pickwickians occupied. They remain as Dickens described them, even in some cases to the very bedsteads and furniture, and are still shown to the interested visitor.

"Winkle's bedroom is inside mine," is how Mr. Tupman put it. That is to say, the one led out of the other, and they are numbered 13 and 19; but which is which no one knows. Number 18, by the way, is the room the Queen slept in on the occasion of her visit, eight months after the appearance of the first part of Pickwick.

Number 17 is claimed as Mr. Pickwick's room, which is also the one Dickens occupied on one occasion, and the one spoken of in Seven Poor Travellers, from which the occupant assured us that after the cathedral bell struck eight he "could smell the delicious savour of turkey and roast beef rising to the window of my adjoining room, which looked down into the yard just where the lights of the kitchen reddened a massive fragment of the castle wall."

An important feature in those days, and presumably to-day, was the ballroom, "the elegant and commodious assembly rooms to the Winglebury Arms." In The Pickwick Papers Dickens thus describes it: "It was a long room, with crimson-covered benches, and wax candles in glass chandeliers. The musicians were securely confined in an elevated den, and quadrilles were being systematically got through by two or three sets of dancers. Two card tables were made up in the adjoining card-room, and two pair of old ladies and a corresponding number of stout gentlemen were executing whist therein."

The room itself is little altered; although the glass chandeliers have been removed, there still remains at the end the veritable elevated den where the fiddlers fiddled. During the war it was turned into a dining-room on account of the military and naval demands of the town; but there may come a time when it will revert to its old glory and tradition.

On the evening of the Pickwickians' arrival Jingle remarks that there is a "Devil of a mess on the staircase, waiter. Forms going up – carpenters coming down – lamps, glasses, harps. What's going forward?"

"Ball, sir," said the waiter.

"Assembly, eh?"

"No, sir, not assembly, sir. Ball for the benefit of charity, sir."

This was the famous ball at which the incident occurred resulting in the challenge to a duel between

Dr. Slammer and Winkle, the details of which require no reiteration here.

But the pleasant fact remains that the Bull Inn exists to-day and the Dickens tradition clings to it still. One instinctively goes there as the centre of the Dickensian atmosphere with which the old city of Rochester is permeated.

The Bull Inn should never lose its fame. Indeed, as long as it lasts it never will, because Pickwick can never be forgotten. The present-day traveller will go by rail, or some day by an aerial bus, and may forget the old days during his journey; but when he arrives there and walks into the inn yard, whole visions of the coaching days will come back to him, and prominent amongst them will be the arrival of the "Commodore" coach with the Pickwickians on board, and the departure of the chaise with the same company with Winkle struggling with the tall mare, on their way to Dingley Dell, which resulted so disastrously. He might be curious enough to want to discover the "little roadside public-house with two elm trees, horse-trough and a sign-post in front," where the travellers attempted to put up the horse. That, however, has not been discovered, although Dickens no doubt had a particular one in his mind at the time.

During their stay at Manor Farm, Dingley Dell, the Pickwickians visited Muggleton to witness the cricket match between Dingley Dell and all Muggleton. "Everybody whose genius has a topographical bent," says Dickens, "knows perfectly well that Muggleton is a corporate town, with a mayor, burgesses and freeman," but so far no topographer has discovered which corporate town it was. Some say Maidstone, others Town Malling. Until that vexed question has been settled, however, the identification of the "large inn with a sign-post in front, displaying an object very common in art, but very rarely met with in nature – to wit, a Blue Lion with three legs in the air, balancing himself on the extreme point of the centre claw of his fourth foot," cannot definitely be verified. The same remark applies to the Crown Inn, where Jingle stopped on the same occasion.

At Maidstone there is a "White Lion," and at Town Malling there is the "Swan." Which of these is the original of the inn where Mr. Wardle hired a chaise and four to pursue Jingle and Miss Rachael, and on whose steps, the following Christmas, the Pickwickians, on their second visit to Dingley Dell, were deposited "high and dry, safe and sound, hale and hearty," by the Muggleton Telegraph, when they discovered the Fat Boy just aroused from a sleep in front of the tap-room fire, must be left to the choice of the reader.

Chapter IV

THE "WHITE HART," BOROUGH
✻✻✻

The pursuit of Jingle and Miss Wardle by the lady's father and Mr. Pickwick, culminates in the "White Hart," which, in days gone by, was one of the most famous of the many famous inns that then stood in the borough of Southwark. Long before Dickens began to write, the "White Hart" was the centre of the coaching activity of the metropolis south of the Thames, and was one of the oldest inns in the country.

Travellers from the Continent and the southern and eastern counties of England to London made it their halting-place, whilst from a business standpoint it had scarcely a rival. Coaches laden with passengers and wagons full of articles of commerce made the courtyard of the inn always a bustling and busy corner of a hustling and busy neighbourhood. In the coaching era, therefore, the "White Hart" was a household word to travellers and business men. Dickens, with his magic pen and inventive genius, made it a household word to the inhabitants of the whole globe, who never had occasion to visit it either for business or pleasure.

Its history goes back many centuries, as far back as 1400, and possibly earlier than that. Its sign was taken from the badge of Richard II, who adopted the emblem of the "White Hart" from the crest of his mother, Joanna of Kent. A fine old inn of the highest type, the "White Hart" no doubt was the resort of the most prominent nobles and retainers of the time, public men of the period and ambassadors of commerce. It is not surprising, therefore, that it figures in English history generally, and was particularly mentioned by Shakespeare. It certainly was the centre of many a stirring scene, and events of feasting and jollity, besides being a place where great trade was transacted.

It is often mentioned in the Paston Letters in reference to Jack Cade, who made it his headquarters in 1450. In Hall's Chronicles it is recorded that the Captain, being made aware of the King's absence, came first to Southwark, and there lodged at the "White Hart." In Henry VI, Part II, Jack Cade is made to say, "Hath my sword therefore broke through London gates, that you should leave me at the 'White Hart' in Southwark?"

Thomas Cromwell, Henry VIII's most able minister, was also associated with the borough of Southwark, and on one occasion (in 1529) it is recorded that he received a message to the effect that one R. awaited him at the "White Hart" on important business. Again the inn has mention in connection with the rebellion brought about by Archbishop Laud's attitude to the Scottish and Puritan Churches, when we are told that the populace and soldiers associated with it lodged at the "White Hart." And in a like manner mention might be made of other occasions during which, in those far-off days, the "White Hart" played some notable part in history and in the social round of the period.

In 1676 it was entirely destroyed by the great fire of Southwark, but was rebuilt immediately afterward on the old site and on the old model. It was described by Strype about this time as a very large inn, and we believe that it was able to accommodate between one and two hundred guests and their retinue, with ample rooms left for their belongings, horses and goods. It did a considerable trade and was esteemed one of the best inns in Southwark, and so it continued as a favourite place of resort for coaches and carriers until the end of the coaching days.

When, therefore, Mr. Pickwick set all the world agog with his adventures, the "White Hart" was recognized as a typical old English inn, and was really at its best. It had arrived at this prosperous state by easy stages during its previous 180 years, and had a reputation for comfort and generous hospitality during the best days of the coaching era, which had reached the golden age when Mr. Pickwick discovered Sam Weller cleaning boots in its coach yard one historic morning in the early nineteenth century.

It is not to be wondered at, then, that Dickens, who knew this district so well and intimately, should introduce the "White Hart" into his book as a setting for one of his most amusing scenes. After speaking of London's inns in general, he makes special mention of those in the Borough, where, he says, there still remained some half-dozen old inns, "which have preserved their external features unchanged, and which have escaped alike the rage for public improvement and the encroachments of private speculation." Since these words were written public improvement has "improved" all of them, except one, the "George," right out of existence.

But let us use Dickens's own words to describe these inns in general and the "White Hart" in particular, for none of ours can improve his picture.

"Great, rambling, queer old places they are, with galleries and passages and staircases, wide enough and antiquated enough to furnish materials for a hundred ghost stories, supposing we should ever be reduced to the lamentable necessity of inventing any, and that the world should exist long enough to exhaust the innumerable veracious legends connected with old London Bridge and its adjacent neighbourhood on the Surrey side.

"It was in the yard of one of these inns – of no less celebrated a one than the 'White Hart' – that a man was busily employed in brushing the dirt off a pair of boots, early on the morning succeeding the events narrated in the last chapter. He was habited in a coarse-striped waistcoat, with black calico sleeves, and blue glass buttons, drab breeches and leggings. A bright red handkerchief was wound in a very loose and unstudied style round his neck, and an old white hat was carelessly thrown on one side of his head. There were two rows of boots before him, one cleaned and the other dirty, and at every addition he made to the clean row, he paused from his work, and contemplated its results with evident satisfaction."

This, we need hardly say, was the inimitable Sam Weller, and it was his first introduction to the story with which his name is now inseparable.

Dickens then goes on to give further particulars of how the yard looked on the particular morning of which he writes:

"The yard presented none of that bustle and activity which are the usual characteristics of a large coach inn. Three or four lumbering wagons, each with a pile of goods beneath its ample canopy, about the height of the second-floor window of an ordinary house, were stowed away beneath a lofty roof which extended over one end of the yard; and another, which was probably to commence its journey that morning, was drawn out into the open space. A double tier of bedroom galleries, with old, clumsy balustrades, ran round two sides of the straggling area, and a double row of bells to correspond, sheltered from the weather by a little sloping roof, hung over the door. . . . Two or three gigs and chaise-carts were wheeled up under different little sheds and penthouses; and the occasional heavy tread of a carthorse or rattling of a chain at the further end of the yard announced to anybody who cared about the matter that the stable lay in that direction. When we add that a few boys in smock frocks were lying asleep on heavy packages, woolpacks and other articles that were scattered about on heaps of straw, we have described as fully as need be the general appearance of the yard of the White Hart Inn, High Street, Borough, on the particular morning in question."

This was the inn, then, to which Mr. Pickwick and Mr. Wardle came in search of the runaway couple, and Sam Weller was the first person they interviewed on the subject. The reader will refer to Chapter X of the book should he want his memory refreshed regarding the amusing scene with Sam, which has been so faithfully pictured by Phiz in one of his illustrations. How they discovered the misguided Rachael, how they bought off the adventurer, Jingle, and how Mr. Pickwick, Wardle and the deserted lady set forth the next day by the Muggleton heavy coach is duly set forth in Dickens's own way.

The "White Hart" remained very much as Dickens found it and described it in 1836 until it was finally demolished in 1889. Following the advent of railways it lost a good deal of its glamour, and in its last years the old galleries on two of its sides were let out in tenements, and the presence of the occupants gave a certain animation to the scene. In the large inner yard were some quaint old house which were crowded with lodgers, but it still hung on to its old traditions of the coaching times, and even up to its last days the old inn was the halting-place of the last of the old-fashioned omnibuses which plied between London Bridge and Clapham.

Nothing now remains to remind us of the old inn which Dickens and Sam Weller have made immortal in the annals of coaching but a narrow turning bearing its name, where is established a Sam Weller Club.

Chapter V

"LA BELLE SAUVAGE" AND THE "MARQUIS OF GRANBY," DORKING
✱✱✱

"La Belle Sauvage" has, like many other historic inns, gone into the limbo of past, if not of forgotten, things, leaving nothing but its name denoting a cul-de-sac, to remind the present generation of its one-time fame.

This was the inn where Tony Weller, resplendent in many layers of cloth cape and huge brimmed hat, stopped "wen he drove up" on the box seat of one of the stage coaches of the period. For Tony was, as everybody knows, a coachman typical of the period of the book, and the "Belle Savage" (the spelling of "savage" here follows the fashion of the period referred to) was where he started and ended his journeys in London. But the anecdote related by his son of how he was hoodwinked into taking out a licence to marry Mrs. Clarke contains the chief of the only two actual references to the fact that his head-quarters were the "Belle Savage," as he called it. It is certainly recorded that he started from the "Bull" in Whitechapel when he drove the Pickwickians to Ipswich, but it is the "Belle Savage" that is associated with his name.

"'What's your name, sir?' says the lawyer.

"'Tony Weller,' says my father. 'Parish?' says the lawyer. 'Belle Savage,' says my father; for he stopped there wen he drove up, and he know'd nothing about parishes, he didn't."

Now it seems to us a curious fact that Dickens never made any further use of this famous inn, either in Pickwick or in his other books; indeed, we can only recall one other reference to it, and that when Sam's father rather despondently told him that "a thousand things may have happened by the time you next hears any news of the celebrated Mr. Veller o' the 'Bell Savage.'" It is particularly curious in regard to Pickwick, for the inn was not only close to the Fleet Prison, which figures so prominently in the book, but its outbuildings actually adjoined it. Meagre as is the reference, it is, nevertheless, retained in the memory, and the inn proclaimed a Pickwickian one with as much satisfaction as if it had been the scene of many an incident such as connect others with the book.

Unfortunately there are only one or two landmarks remaining to show that it ever existed. One of these is the archway out of Ludgate Hill, just beyond the hideous bridge which runs across the road, at the side of No. 68, which in Pickwickian days was No. 38. Perhaps the shape of the yard which still bears the inn's name may be considered as a trace of its former glory. This yard is now surrounded by the business premises of Messrs. Cassell and Co., the well-known publishers, which occupy the whole site of the old building.

We can find no earlier reference to the inn than that in the reign of Henry VI, when a certain John French in a deed (1453) made over to his mother for her life "all that tenement or inn, with its appurtenances, called Savage's Inn, otherwise called 'le Bell on the Hope' in the parish of Fleet Street, London." Prior to that it may be surmised that it belonged to a citizen of the name of Savage, probably the "William Savage of Fleet Street in the Parish of St. Bridget," upon whom, it is recorded in 1380, an attempt was made "to obtain by means of forged letter, twenty shillings."

It would be clear from this that its sign was the "Bell and Hoop," before it became the property of the Savage family, from whom there can be no doubt it got its name of "La Belle Savage." According to Stow, Mrs. Isabella Savage gave the inn to the Cutlers' Company, but this would seem to be incorrect, for more recent research has proved definitely that it was a John Craythorne who did so in 1568. The crest of the Cutlers' Company is the Elephant and Castle, and a stone bas-relief of it, which once stood over the gateway of the inn under the sign of the Bell, is still to be seen on the east wall of La Belle Savage

Yard to-day. It was placed there some fifty years ago when the old inn was demolished.

Years before Craythorne presented the inn to the Cutlers' Company, however, it was known as "La Belle Sauvage," for we are told that Sir Thomas Wyatt, the warrior poet, in 1554 made his last stand with his Kentish men against the troops of Mary just in front of the ancient inn, "La Belle Sauvage." He was attempting to capture Ludgate and was driven back with some thousands of rebel followers to Temple Bar, where he surrendered himself to Sir Maurice Berkeley, and so sealed his own fate and that of poor Lady Jane Grey.

Again, in 1584, the inn was described as "Ye Belle Sauvage," and there have been many speculations as to the origin of the name, and some doubt as to the correct spelling.

In 1648 and 1672 exhibitions of landlords' tokens of various inns were held, whereat were shown two belonging to "La Belle Sauvage," the sign of one being that of an Indian woman holding a bow and arrow, and the other, of Queen Anne's time, that of a savage standing by a bell, and it has been conjectured that this latter sign may have suggested the name. But as the inn was known as "Ye Belle Savage" some sixty years previously this is hardly likely. Another conjecture as to its origin was made by Addison in

The Spectator, who, having read an old French romance which gives an account of a beautiful woman called in French "La Belle Sauvage" and translated into English as "Bell Savage," considered the name was derived from that source. Alderman Sir W. P. Treloar, in his excellent little book on "Ludgate Hill," puts forth another idea. "As the inn," he says, "was the mansion of the Savage family, and near to Bailey or Ballium, it is at least conceivable that it would come to be known as the Bail or Bailey Savage Inn, and afterward the Old Bail or Bailey Inn." We prefer, however, to favour the Isabella Savage theory as the likely one.

Long before Elizabeth's time and long after-wards the inn was a very famous one. In the days before Shakespeare the actors gave performances of their plays in the old inn yard, using the courtyards as the pit in theatres is used to-day, and the upper and lower galleries for what are now the boxes and galleries of modern theatres. In 1556, the old inns, such as the "Cross Keys," the "Bull" and "Belle Sauvage" were used extensively for this purpose, the latter, we are told, almost ranking as a permanent theatre. We find Collier also stating that the "Belle Sauvage" was a favourite place for these performances.

Originally the old inn consisted of two courts, an inner and outer one. The present archway from Ludgate Hill led into the latter, which at one time contained private houses. A distinguished resident in one of these (No. 11) was Grinling Gibbons. According to Horace Walpole, Gibbons carved an exquisite pot of flowers in wood, which stood on his window-sill there, and shook surprisingly with the motion of the coaches that passed beneath. The inn proper, surrounded by its picturesque galleries, stood in a corner of the inner court, entered by a second archway about halfway up the yard.

Part of the inn abutted on to the back of Fleet Prison, and Mr. Tearle in his Rambles with an American, bearing this fact in mind, ingeniously suggests that the conception of the idea for smuggling Mr. Pickwick from the prison by means of a piano without works may have been conceived in Mr. Weller's brain while resting in the "Belle Sauvage" and contemplating the prison wall.

In 1828, the period of The Pickwick Papers, J. Pollard painted a picture of the Cambridge coach ("The Star") leaving the inn. A portion of this picture showing the coach and the north side of Ludgate Hill, was published as a lithograph by Thomas McLean of the Haymarket. It gives the details of the inn entrance and the coach on a large scale. The inn at the time was owned by Robert Nelson. He was a son of Mrs. Ann Nelson, the popular proprietor of the "Bull," Whitechapel. Besides the coaches for the eastern counties, those also for other parts of the country started from its precincts, for such names as Bath, Bristol, Exeter, Plymouth, Oxford, Gloucester, Coventry, Carlisle, Manchester were announced on the signboard at the side of the archway.

In spite of the fact that Dickens only once refers to the inn, its name and fame, nevertheless, will always be associated with him and with Tony Weller, who was so familiar with it and so attached to it, as to name it as the parish he resided in.

The relating of the story of how Tony Weller was driven into his second marriage, which reveals "La Belle Sauvage" as his headquarters, also first brings into prominence the "Markis o' Granby," Dorking, as the residence of Mrs. Susan Clarke, and incidentally the scene of more than one amusing incident after she became Mrs. Weller, senior. "The 'Marquis of Granby' in Mrs. Weller's time," we are informed, "was quite a model of a roadside public-house of the better class – just large enough to be convenient, and small enough to be snug."

In the chapter describing how Sam displayed his high sense of duty as a son, by paying a visit to his "mother-in-law," as he called her, and how he discovered Mr. Stiggins indulging in "hot pine-apple rum and water," we get a little pen-picture of the inn.

"On the opposite side of the road was a signboard on a high post representing the head and shoulders of a gentleman with an apoplectic countenance, in a red coat with deep blue facings, and a touch of the same over his three-cornered hat, for a sky . . . an undoubted likeness of the Marquis of Granby of glorious memory. The bar window displayed a choice collection of geranium plants, and a well-dusted row of spirit phials. The open shutters bore a variety of golden inscriptions, eulogistic of good beds and neat wines; and the choice group of countrymen and hostlers lounging about the stable door and horse-trough afforded presumptive proof of the excellent quality of the ale and spirits which were sold within."

Phiz's picture, forming the vignette on the title-page, hardly does justice to this description, although the incident of old Weller performing the "beautiful and exhilarating" act of immersing Mr. Stiggins's head in the horse-trough full of water, is spirited enough.

The "Markis Gran by Dorken," as the elder Weller styled it in his letter to Sam, is another of those inns, which figure prominently in the book, that have never been actually identified. Robert Allbut, in 1897, claimed to have found the original in the High Street opposite the Post Office at the side of Chequers' Court. Only a part of it then existed, and was being used as a grocer's shop.

Herbert Railton gave an artistic picture of the courtyard in the Jubilee edition of the book, but we are not able to state on what authority it was based.

There were, however, two inns at Dorking, the "King's Head" and the "King's Arms," over which speculation has been rife as to which was the original of the inn so favoured by the Revd. Mr. Stiggins. Of the two, perhaps, the latter, still existing, seems to fit Dickens's description best.

Chapter VI

THE "LEATHER BOTTLE," COBHAM, KENT
✱✱✱

The charming Kentish village of Cobham was familiar to Dickens in his early boyhood days, as was the whole delightful countryside surrounding it. That he loved it throughout his whole life there is ample evidence in his letters. It was inevitable, therefore, that his enthusiasm for it should find vent in his stories, and the first references to its green woods and green shady lanes are to be found in charming phrases in The Pickwick Papers, with the "Leather Bottle" as the centre of attraction.

The inn is first named in the book in Mr. Tupman's pathetic letter to Mr. Pickwick written on a certain historic morning at Dingley Dell:

"MY DEAR PICKWICK,

"You, my dear friend, are placed far beyond the reach of many mortal frailties and weaknesses which ordinary people cannot over come. You do not know what it is, at one blow, to be deserted by a lovely and fascinating creature, and to fall a victim to the artifices of a villain, who hid the grin of cunning beneath the mask of friendship.

I hope you never may. Any letter, addressed to me at the 'Leather Bottle,' Cobham, Kent, will be forwarded – supposing I still exist. I hasten from the sight of the world, which has become odious to me. Should I hasten from it altogether, pity – forgive me. Life, my dear Pickwick, has become insupportable to me. The spirit which burns within us, is a porter's knot, on which to rest the heavy load of worldly cares and troubles; and when that spirit fails us, the burden is too heavy to be borne. We sink beneath it. You may tell Rachel – Ah, that name!

"TRACY TUPMAN."

No sooner had Mr. Pickwick read this plaintive missive than he decided to follow, with his two other companions, Winkle and Snodgrass, in search of their depressed friend. On the coach journey to Rochester "the violence of their grief had sufficiently abated to admit of their making a very excellent early dinner," and having discovered the right road all three set forward again in the after-noon to walk to Cobham.

"A delightful walk it was; for it was a pleasant afternoon in June, and their way lay through a deep and shady wood, cooled by the light wind which gently rustled the thick foliage, and enlivened by the songs of the birds that perched upon the boughs. The ivy and the moss crept in thick clusters over the old trees, and the soft green turf overspread the ground like a silken mat. They emerged upon an open park, with an ancient hall, displaying the quaint and picturesque architecture of Elizabeth's time. Long vistas of stately oaks and elm trees appeared on every side; large herds of deer were cropping the fresh grass; and occasionally a startled hare scoured along the ground, with the speed of the shadows thrown by the light clouds which sweep across a sunny landscape like a passing breath of summer."

Dickens wrote that charming descriptive passage in 1836, probably whilst spending his honeymoon at Chalk near by, and anyone taking the same walk will find that the words paint the scene perfectly and faithfully to-day, so unspoiled and unaltered is it. The spot will delight the traveler as much as it did Mr. Pickwick, who exclaimed, as it all came in view: "If this were the place to which all who are troubled with our friend's complaint came, I fancy their old attachment to this world would very soon return"; at any rate, his other companions were all agreed upon the point. "And really," added Mr. Pickwick, after half an hour's walking had brought them to the village, "really for a misanthrope's choice, this is one of the prettiest and most desirable places of residence I ever met with."

Having been directed to the "Leather Bottle," "a clean and commodious village ale-house," the three travellers entered, and at once inquired for a gentleman of the name of Tupman. In those days the inn was managed by a landlady, who promptly told Tom to "show the gentlemen into the parlour."

"A stout country lad opened the door at the end of the passage, and the three friends entered a long, low-roofed room, furnished with a large number of high-backed, leather-cushioned chairs, of fantastic shapes, and embellished with a great variety of old portraits and roughly coloured prints of some antiquity. At the upper end of the room was a table, with a white cloth upon it, well covered with a roast fowl, bacon, ale and et ceteras; and at the table sat Mr. Tupman, looking as unlike a man who had taken his leave of the world as possible.

"On the entrance of his friends, that gentleman laid down his knife and fork, and with a mournful air advanced to meet them."

Mr. Tupman was quite affected by his friends' anxiety for his welfare, but any demonstration was nipped in the bud by Mr. Pickwick's insisting on Mr. Tupman finishing his delicate repast first. At the conclusion thereof, Mr. Pickwick, "having refreshed himself with a copious draft of ale," conducted poor Tracy to the churchyard opposite, and pacing to and fro eventually combated his companion's resolution with a successfully eloquent appeal to him once again to join his friends.

On their way back to the inn, Mr. Pickwick made that great discovery "which had been the pride and boast of his friends, and the envy of every antiquarian in this or any other country," of a small broken stone, partially buried in the ground in front of a cottage door, which, as everybody knows, bore the inscription:

```
      - | -
    B I L S T
      U M
    P S H I
      S.M.
     A R K
```

The exultation and joy of the Pickwickians knew no bounds and they carefully carried the important stone into the inn, where Mr. Pickwick's eyes sparkled with a delight as he sat and gloated over the treasure he had discovered, the detailed adventure with which need not be related here. Having carefully packed his prize, its discovery and the happy meeting were duly celebrated in an evening of festivity and conversation.

"It was past 11 o'clock – a late hour for the little village of Cobham – when Mr. Pickwick retired to the bedroom which had been prepared for his reception. He threw open the lattice-window, and, setting his light upon the table, fell into a train of meditation on the hurried events of the two preceding days.

"The hour and the place were both favourable to contemplation; Mr. Pickwick was roused by the church clock striking twelve. The first stroke of the hour sounded solemnly in his ear, but when the bell ceased the stillness seemed insupportable; he almost felt as if he had lost a companion. He was nervous and excited; and hastily undressing himself, and placing his light in the chimney, got into bed."

But Mr. Pickwick could not sleep following the excitement of the day's adventure, so "after half an hour's tumbling about, he came to the unsatisfactory conclusion that it was of no use trying to sleep, so he got up and partially dressed himself. Anything, he thought, was better than lying there fancying all kinds of horrors. He looked out of the window – it was very dark. He walked about the room – it was very lonely."

Suddenly he thought of The Madman's Manuscript which he had brought from Dingley Dell, and, trimming his light, he put on his spectacles and composed himself to read that blood-curdling narrative. On reaching the end, Mr. Pickwick's candle "went suddenly out" and he once more scrambled into bed.

Next morning, with the coveted antiquarian treasure, the four gentlemen travelled to London by coach.

That is the story of the association of the "Leather Bottle," Cobham, with The Pickwick Papers, which has spread its fame to the uttermost parts of the world. That is the chief reason why in certain seasons of the year the "Leather Bottle" and Cobham are visited by thousands of admirers of the novelist, and also why the ideal Kentish village has become a magnet to lovers of England's rural lanes and arable fields; but the charm of it all is that when it is reached both it and the inn are to be found exactly as Dickens so faithfully described them many years ago.

The inn is just an inn; a commodious village alehouse; that is the best description of it. Its picturesque exterior, with its hanging sign bearing a portrait of Mr. Pickwick in the act of addressing the club, and the legend, "Dickens's Old Pickwick Leather Bottle," and its red-tiled roof, its small windows with their old-fashioned shutters, is no less quaint and attractive than its old-time interior. Its original sign – the Leather Bottle – hangs in the tiny bar which is on the immediate right of the passage, and behind a glass window, looking as unlike a bar as anything imaginable. From this curious little receptacle refreshment for travellers and villagers is dispensed in stone mugs embellished with the sign of the inn; and its "low-roofed room" is at the end of the passage as Mr. Pickwick found it, with its oak beams across the ceiling adding to its picturesqueness. In this room the "high back leather-cushioned chairs" are still to be seen, together with a grandfather clock and other antique pieces of furniture in thorough keeping with tradition.

There, too, is the great "variety of old portraits" which decorated the wall in Mr. Pickwick's time, with every other available inch of wall space now covered with portraits of the novelist and his memorable characters, pictures of scenes from his books, Dickensian relics and knicknacks, either associated with the book which brought it fame or with other books of the famous Boz. In a word, it is a veritable Dickens museum, in which every lover of the novelist lingers with pleasure and amazement, oblivious of the fact that possibly his tea is getting cold.

Here the visitor can have his meal as did Mr. Tupman, not perhaps in such solitude, for the "Leather Bottle" to-day is often a busy centre for pedestrians from the neighbouring villages, and cyclists and motorists from far-distant towns and cities.

Upstairs, overlooking the churchyard, is the identical front bedroom where Mr. Pickwick spent the night, and where he sat reading long into the early and eerie hours of the morning. The present landlord is a true

Dickensian in knowledge and character, and endeavours to make everybody comfortable and welcome, no matter who he be. A glance at the visitors' book will show how the inn has been sought out by every grade of society from all over the world. Indeed, we doubt if Shakespeare's birthplace can surpass this inn in popularity.

But it is not merely a Pickwickian inn. It is a Dickensian inn for which the novelist himself had a warm place in his heart for its own sake, spending many pleasant hours within its comfortable walls. Long before he came to live at Gad's Hill, close by, he loved the place. As a boy at Chatham, probably he walked over in company with his father; and when spending his honeymoon at Chalk, he no doubt roamed in the beautiful lanes around the village. In 1840, after spending a vacation at Broadstairs, he posted back to London with Maclise and Forster by way of Chatham, Rochester and Cobham, and the three spent two agreeable days in revisiting well-remembered scenes.

Again in 1841 Dickens and Forster passed a day and night in Cobham and its neighbourhood, sleeping at the "Leather Bottle," and when he ultimately became a resident at Gad's Hill the whole district was the greatest pleasure to him. His biographer, writing of the year 1856, says: "Round Cobham, skirting the park and village and passing the 'Leather Bottle,' famous in the pages of Pickwick, was a favourite walk with Dickens."

He would often take his friends and visitors with him on these walks, and would never miss the old village inn. W. P. Frith has told us of how, when he formed one of the party on one of these occasions, "we went to the 'Leather Bottle,'" and, no doubt, the company was merry and reminiscent on the association of the village with the novelist and his immortal book.

The happy thing to be remembered to-day is that neither the village, park, nor inn have changed since those historic days, so that little imagination is required by the pilgrim to recall to his mind the scenes and characters which have made them familiar to lovers of Dickens in every English-speaking country.

Chapter VII

THE "TOWN ARMS," EATANSWILL, AND THE INN OF "THE BAGMAN'S STORY"
***

Following the Pickwickians in the sequence of their peregrinations, we become confronted with the problem, "which was the prototype of Eatanswill?" Having weighed the evidence of each of the other claimants for the honour, we favour that of Sudbury in Suffolk, for which so good a case has been presented. That being so, the "Rose and Crown" undoubtedly would be the original of the "Town Arms," the headquarters of the Blues and the inn at which Mr. Pickwick and his friends alighted on their arrival in the town.

First let us briefly state the case for Sudbury.

In the opening paragraph of Chapter XIII of the book, Dickens writes:

"We will frankly acknowledge, that up to the period of our being first immersed in the voluminous papers of the Pickwick Club, we had never heard of Eatanswill; we will with equal candour admit, that we have in vain searched for proof of the actual existence of such a place at the present day. . . . We are therefore led to believe, that Mr. Pickwick, with that anxious desire to abstain from giving offence to any, and with those delicate feelings for which all who knew him well know he was so eminently remarkable, purposely substituted a fictitious designation, for the real name of the place in which his observations were made. We are confirmed in this belief by a little circumstance, apparently slight and trivial in itself, but when considered from this point of view, not undeserving of notice. In Mr. Pickwick's notebook, we can just trace an entry of the fact, that the places of himself and followers were booked by the Norwich coach; but this entry was afterwards lined through, as if for the purpose of concealing even the direction in which the borough is situated."

That description fits Sudbury admirably and faithfully, but does not by any means fit either Ipswich or Norwich, the two other claimants, and the evidence of Mr. C. Finden Waters, a one-time proprietor of the "Rose and Crown" at Sudbury, makes it almost certain that Sudbury was the place Dickens had in mind.

Mr. Waters, in 1906, devoted much time and research in order to establish his claim, and in March, 1907, read a paper, setting forth in detail the various points which led him to that conclusion, to the members of a then newly formed coterie who called themselves "The Eatanswill Club." It appears that this evidence established the fact that Dickens visited Sudbury in 1834. On the 25th and 26th July in the same year, a

Parliamentary by-election took place there, the incidents of which, as reported by the Essex Standard of that period, coincided remarkably with those recorded in connexion with the "Eatanswill" election in The Pickwick Papers. In 1835, Dickens visited Ipswich for The Morning Chronicle, and reported the election at that place. It is now tolerably certain that he went on to Sudbury for a similar purpose.

A further point is, Mr. Pickwick left by the Norwich coach. "Eatanswill," as we have seen, being a small borough near Bury St. Edmunds, and on the Norwich coach route, as was Sudbury, the latter's claim gains strength indeed, if it does not actually settle the question. At any rate, no other small borough could be named with any assurance that Dickens had it in his mind. Indeed, in the year 1834, there were only four Parliamentary boroughs in Suffolk, viz. Sudbury, Ipswich, Bury St. Edmunds and Eye. Ipswich, Mr. Pickwick visited AFTER the "Eatanswill" election, and does not hesitate to describe it under its right name. Moreover, the claims of Ipswich have been relinquished by even local literary men, who in 1905 actually proved that town to be topographically impossible and named Sudbury as the original. Bury St. Edmunds is the place to which Mr. Pickwick travelled AFTER leaving "Eatanswill," and as that borough figures prominently in the book undisguised, it cannot be that. Eye is off the Norwich coach road, and no one has ever suggested that it has any claim to the honour. Sudbury alone, therefore, remains as presenting all the main features required for the original.

In 1834 the "Rose and Crown," Sudbury, was the headquarters of the "Blue" candidate, and so its claim to be the original of the "Town Arms," Eatanswill, would seem to be well made out; and so serious and certain were the citizens of Sudbury on the point that they established an "Eatanswill Club" there, and revived the Eatanswill Gazette devoted to "Pickwickian, Dickensian and Eatanswillian humour and research."

Accepting this evidence, we naturally assume the "Rose and Crown" to be the "Town Arms," which, late in the evening, Mr. Pickwick and his companions, assisted by Sam, dismounting from the roof of the Eatanswill coach, entered through an excited crowd assembled there. They found, however, the inn had no accommodation to offer, but through the friendliness of Mr. Pott, Mr. Pickwick and Winkle accompanied that gentleman to his home, whilst Mr. Tupman, Mr. Snodgrass and Sam repaired to the "Peacock." They all first dined together at the "Town Arms" and arranged to reassemble there in the morning. It was here the barmaid was reported to have been bribed to "hocus the brandy and water of fourteen unpolled electors as was a stopping in the house," and where most of the exciting scenes of the election either took place, or had their rise in its precincts.

On the same authority we locate the "Swan" as being the original of the "Peacock," the headquarters of the "buffs," where Tupman and Snodgrass lodged, and where was told the Bagman's story which brings us up against yet another problem – "which was the inn on Marlborough Downs that plays so important a part in that narrative?"

We think, however, Mr. Charles G. Harper has solved the knotty point in his valuable book The Old Inns of Old England. He comes to the conclusion, by a process of elimination, that the "Waggon and Horses" at Beckhampton, which exists to-day, nearly realises the description of the inn given in the story. "It is," he says, "just the house a needy bagman such as Tom Smart would have selected. It was in coaching days a homely yet comfortable inn, that received those travellers who did not relish either the state or the expense of the great Beckhampton Inn opposite, where post-horses were kept, and where the very elite of the roads resorted."

If its comfort, as described in the following paragraph, is to-day equal to that found by Tom Smart, it is a place to seek for personal pleasure, as well as a Pickwickian landmark.

"In less than five minutes' time, Tom was ensconced in the room opposite the bar – the very room where he had imagined the fire blazing – before a substantial matter-of-fact roaring fire, composed of something short of a bushel of coals, and wood enough to make half a dozen decent gooseberry bushes, piled half-way up the chimney, and roaring and crackling with a sound that of itself would have warmed the heart of any reasonable man. This was comfortable, but this was not all, for a smartly dressed girl, with a bright eye and a neat ankle, was laying a very clean white cloth on the table; and as Tom sat with his slippered feet on the fender, and his back to the open door, he saw a charming prospect of the bar reflected in the glass over the chimney-piece, with delightful rows of green bottles and gold labels, together with jars of pickles and preserves, and cheeses and boiled hams, and rounds of beef, arranged on shelves in the most tempting and delicious array. Well, that was comfortable, too; but even this was not all – for in the bar, seated at tea at the nicest possible little table, drawn close up before the brightest possible little fire, was a buxom widow of somewhere about eight-and-forty or thereabouts, with a face as comfortable as the bar, who was evidently the landlady of the house, and the supreme ruler over all these agreeable possessions."

What happened afterwards is another story. Many other incidents occurred at Eatanswill during the Pickwickians' stay there, the narration of which is not our purpose in these pages. One, however, led Sam and his master hurriedly to leave the town on a certain morning in pursuit of Alfred Jingle, who had put in an appearance at Mrs. Leo Hunter's fancy-dress fete, and on seeing Mr. Pickwick there, had as quickly left if as he had entered it. Mr. Pickwick, on enquiry, discovering that Alfred Jingle, alias Charles Fitz Marshall, was residing at the "Angel," Bury, set off in hot haste to hunt him down, determined to prevent him from deceiving anyone else as he had deceived him; and so we follow him in the next chapter.

Chapter VIII

THE "ANGEL," BURY ST. EDMUNDS
***

"Beg your pardon, sir, is this Bury St. Edmunds?"

The words were addressed by Sam Weller to Mr. Pickwick as the two sat on top of a coach as it "rattled through the well-paved streets of a handsome little town, of thriving appearance." Eventually stopping before "a large inn situated in a wide street, nearly facing the old Abbey," Mr. Pickwick, looking up, added, "'and this is the "Angel." We alight here, Sam. But some caution is necessary. Order a private room, and do not mention my name. You understand?'"

"'Right as a trivet, sir,' replied Mr. Weller, with a wink of intelligence; and having dragged Mr. Pickwick's portmanteau from the hind boot, into which it had been hastily thrown when they joined the coach at Eatanswill, Mr. Weller disappeared on his errand. A private room was speedily engaged; and into it Mr. Pickwick was ushered without delay." Having been settled comfortably therein, partaken of dinner and listened to Sam's philosophy about a good night's rest, he allowed that worthy to go and "worm ev'ry secret out o' the boots' heart" regarding the whereabouts of Fitz Marshall, as he assured Mr. Pickwick he could do in five minutes. As good as his word he returned with his information that the gentleman in question also had a private room in the "Angel," but was dining out that night and had taken his servant with him. It was accordingly arranged that Sam should have a talk with the said servant in the morning with a view of learning what he could about his master's plans.

"As it appeared that this was the best arrangement that could be made, it was finally agreed upon. Mr. Weller, by his master's permission, retired to spend his evening in his own way; and was shortly afterwards elected, by the unanimous voice of the assembled company, into the tap-room chair, in which honourable post he acquitted himself so much to the satisfaction of the gentlemen-frequenters, that the roars of laughter and approbation penetrated to Mr. Pickwick's bedroom, and shortened the term of his natural rest by at least three hours. Early on the ensuing morning Mr. Weller was dispelling all the feverish remains of the previous evening's conviviality, through the instrumentality of a halfpenny shower-bath (having induced a young gentleman attached to the stable department, by the offer of a coin, to pump over his head and face, until he was perfectly restored), when he was attracted by the appearance of a young fellow in mulberry-coloured livery, who was sitting on a bench in the yard, reading what appeared to be a hymn-book, with an air of deep abstraction, but who occasionally stole a glance at the individual under the pump, as if he took some interest in his proceedings, nevertheless."

This was no other than Job Trotter, the servant to Mr. Alfred Jingle of No Hall, No Where, and in a few moments the two were in animated conversation over a little liquid refreshment at the bar. How Job Trotter and Alfred Jingle not only got the better of the usually astute Sam and the innocent Mr. Pickwick, and entangled the latter into a very embarrassing situation at the Young Ladies' School in the district; and how the latter extricated himself from the awkward predicament only to find that the instigators of it had again hurriedly left the town, is best gathered from the pages of the book itself.

"The process of being washed in the night air, and rough-dried in a closet is as dangerous as it is peculiar." This having been the case with Mr. Pickwick, he suffered as a consequence, and was laid up with an attack of rheumatism, and had to spend a couple of days in his bed at the hotel. To pass away the time, he devoted himself to "editing" the love story of Nathaniel Pipkin, which he read to his friends, who, having by this time arrived at the hotel, gathered at his bedside and took their wine there with him.

It was whilst staying at the "Angel" that Mr. Pickwick received the first intimation that a writ for breach of promise had been issued against him at the instance of Mrs. Bardell, much to the alarm and amusement of his friends. He did not, however, hasten back to London, but accepted Mr. Wardle's invitation to a shooting party in the neighbourhood, where he again involved himself in a further misadventure.

Now all these little untoward events happened whilst Mr. Pickwick was staying at the "Angel," and. not only have they caused much amusement to the readers of the book, but incidentally have added fame and importance to the "Angel" at Bury to such an extent that the faithful reader of Pickwick who finds himself in the neighbourhood would no more think of passing the "Angel" than would the pilgrim to the town omit visiting the famous abbey. He will find the hotel little altered since the day when Mr. Pickwick visited it, either as regards its old-time atmosphere or its Victorian hospitality.

It is a very plain and severe-looking building from the outside, suggesting a gigantic doll's house with real steps up to the front door all complete. Although it does not look as inspiring on approaching it as most Dickensian inns do, its interior, nevertheless, makes up in comfort what its exterior lacks in picturesqueness.

It has stood since 1779 and occupies the site of three ancient inns known at the time as the "Angel," the

"Castle" and the "White Bear," respectively. In such an ancient town as Bury St. Edmunds, with so many years behind it, the "Angel" could tell a story worth narrating. Fronting the gates of the ancient Abbey, it occupies the most prominent place in the town. In the wide space before it the Bury fair was held, and a famous and fashionable festivity it was, which lasted in the olden time for several days. Latterly, however, one day is deemed sufficient, and that is September 21 in each year.

In spite of its sombre appearance from the outside, it is considered one of the most important hotels in West Suffolk, and is still a typical old English inn, "a byword for comfort and generous hospitality throughout the eastern counties." The spacious coffee-room, its well-appointed drawing and sitting-rooms, its many bedrooms, have an appeal to those desiring ease rather than the luxuriousness of the modern style. In addition it has extensive yards and stables, survivals of the old posting days, with a cosy tap-room and bar, to say nothing of all the natural little nooks and corners and accessories which pertain only to old-world hostelries.

There still remains the pump under which Sam had his "halfpenny shower-bath." And in the tap-room one can be easily reminded of the scene over which Sam presided and acquitted himself with so much satisfaction.

As to which was the room occupied by Mr. Pickwick, history is silent; but when Dickens was on his reporting expedition in Suffolk during the electoral campaign of 1835, he stayed at the "Angel" and, tradition says, slept in room No. 11. Mr. Percy FitzGerald, on visiting it some years ago, ventured to seek of the "gnarled" waiter information on the momentous question of Mr. Pickwick and his adventure.

"Piokwick, sir? Why, HE knew all about it," was the reply. "No. 11 was Mr. Pickwick's room, and the proprietor would tell us everything. A most quaint debate arose," says Mr. FitzGerald, "on Mr. Pickwick's stay at the hotel. The host pronounced EX CATHEDRA and without hesitation about the matter. . . . The power and vitality of the Pickwickian legend are extraordinary indeed; all day long we found people bewildered, as it were, by this faith, mixing up the author and his hero."

This is not unusual, and even in these days we find that Dickens's characters have become so real that no one stops to discuss whether this or that really happened to them, but just simply accepts their comings and goings as the comings and goings of the heroes and heroines of history are accepted, with perhaps just a little more belief in them. And so we can be assured that the "Angel" at Bury will be chiefly remembered as the hotel where Mr. Pickwick and his companions stayed, whoever before or since may have honoured it with a visit, or whatever else in its history may be recalled as important.

In 1861 Dickens again visited the town to give his famous readings from his works, and put up at the "Angel," so that the county hotel has many reasons for the proud title of being a Dickensian inn.

Chapter IX

THE "BLACK BOY," CHELMSFORD, THE "MAGPIE AND STUMP," AND THE "BULL," WHITECHAPEL
***

After Mr. Pickwick and Sam had been so cleverly outwitted by Jingle and Job Trotter at Bury, they returned to London. Taking liquid refreshment one day afterwards in a city hostelry they chanced upon the elder Weller, who, in the course of conversation, revealed the fact that, whilst "working" an Ipswich coach, he had taken up Jingle and Job Trotter at the "Black Boy" at Chelmsford: "I took 'em up," he emphasised, "right through to Ipswich, where the manservant – him in the mulberries – told me they was a-going to put up for a long time."

Mr. Pickwick decided to follow them, and started, as will be seen presently, from the Bull Inn, Whitechapel, for that town.

The reference to the "Black Boy" is but a passing one, and it is not even recorded that Mr. Pickwick stopped there on his journey out; but the inn where Jingle was "taken up" was then one of the best known on the Essex road, and was not demolished until 1857, when it was replaced by a modern public-house which still displays the old signboard. In an article in The

Dickensian[1] Mr. G. O. Rickwood gives some interesting particulars concerning its history, from which we gather that originally the "Black Boy" was the town house of the de Veres, the famous Earls of Oxford, whose principal seat, Hedingham Castle, was within a short distance of Chelmsford. It was converted into a hostelry in the middle of the seventeenth century, and was first known as the Crown or New Inn. It was an ancient timber structure house, and some of the carved woodwork, with the well-known device of the boar's head taken from one of the rooms of the old inn, is still preserved in Chelmsford Museum.

At the close of the eighteenth century the "Black Boy" was recognised as the leading hostelry of the town, and was known far and wide. In the Pickwickian days it was a busy posting-house for the coaches from London to many parts of Norfolk.

Before Mr. Pickwick carried out his determination to pursue Jingle, he had occasion to visit the "Magpie and Stump," "situated in a court, happy in the double advantage of being in the vicinity of Clare Market and closely approximating to the back of New Inn." This was the favoured tavern, sacred to the evening orgies of Mr. Lowten and his companions, and by ordinary people would be designated a public-house. The object of Mr. Pickwick's visit was to discover Mr.

---

[1] 1917, p.214.

Lowten, and on enquiry, found him presiding over a sing-song and actually engaged in obliging with a comic song at the moment. After a brief interview with that worthy, Mr. Pickwick was prevailed upon to join the festive party.

There were, at the time, two taverns, either of which might have stood as the original for the "Magpie and Stump"; the "Old Black Jack" and the "George the Fourth," both in Portsmouth Street, and both were demolished in 1896. Which was the one Dickens had in mind it is difficult to say. His description of its appearance runs as follows: "In the lower windows, which were decorated with curtains of a saffron hue, dangled two or three printed cards, bearing reference to Devonshire cyder and Dantzic spruce, while a large blackboard, announcing in white letters to an enlightened public that there were 500,000 barrels of double stout in the cellars of the establishment, left the mind in a state of not unpleasing doubt and uncertainty, as to the precise direction in the bowels of the earth in which this mighty cavern might be supposed to extend. When we add that the weather-beaten signboard bore the half-obliterated semblance of a magpie intently eyeing a crooked streak of brown paint, which the neighbours had been taught from infancy to consider as the 'stump,' we have said all that need be said of the exterior of the edifice."

The "Old Black Jack" has been identified as the original of the "Magpie and Stump" by some topographers, whilst Robert Allbut in his Rambles in Dickens-land favoured the "Old George the Fourth," adding that Dickens and Thackeray were well-remembered visitors there.

The Bull Inn, Whitechapel, the starting-place of Tony Weller's coach which was to take Mr. Pickwick to Ipswich, was actually at No. 25 Aldgate, and was perhaps the most famous of the group of inns of the neighbourhood whence many of the Essex, Suffolk and Norfolk coaches set out on their journeys. At the time of which we write it was owned by Mrs. Ann Nelson, whose antecedents had been born and bred in the business, while she herself had interests in more than one city hostelry, as well as owned coaches.

Mr. Charles G. Harper has several references to, and interesting anecdotes about, Mrs. Ann Nelson and her inns in his "Road" books. In one such reference he tells us Mrs. Ann Nelson was "one of those stern, dignified, magisterial women of business, who were quite a remarkable feature of the coaching age, who saw their husbands off to an early grave and alone carried on the peculiarly exacting double business of inn-keeping and coach-proprietorship, and did so with success." She was the "Napoleon and Caesar" combined of the coaching business. Energetic, she spared neither herself nor her servants. The last to bed she was also the first to rise, "looking after the stable people and seeing that the horses had their feeds and were properly cared for." Insistent as she was on rigid punctuality in all things, and hard as she was on those who served her, she, nevertheless, treated them very well, and gave the coachmen and guards a special room, where they dined as well at reduced prices as any of the coffee-room customers. This room was looked upon as their private property, and there they regaled themselves with the best the house could provide. It was more sacred and exclusive than the commercial-rooms of the old Bagmen days, and was strictly unapproachable by any but those for whom it was set apart.

The "Bull" began to decline when the railway was opened in 1839, and in 1868 it was demolished.

There is no doubt that Dickens knew it well, and probably used it in his journalistic days when having to take journeys to the eastern counties to report election speeches. In The Uncommercial Traveller he speaks of having strolled up to the empty yard of the "Bull," "who departed this life I don't know when, and whose coaches had all gone I don't know where."

When, therefore, he wanted a starting-point for Mr. Pickwick's adventure to Ipswich, the "Bull," which was nothing less than an institution at the time, readily occurred to him.

There is an anecdote about Dickens and the coachmen's private apartment, told by Mr. Charles G. Harper. "On one occasion Dickens had a seat at a table, and 'the Chairman,' after sundry flattering remarks, as a tribute to the novelist's power of describing a coach Journey, said, 'Mr. Dickens, we knows you knows wot's wot, but can you, sir, 'andle a vip?' There was no mock modesty in Dickens. He acknowledged he could describe a journey down the road, but he regretted that in the management of a 'vip' he was not expert."

Here Sam arrived one morning with his master's travelling bag and portmanteau, to be closely followed by Mr. Pickwick himself, who, as Sam told his father, was "cabbin' it . . . havin' two mile o' danger at eightpence." In the inn yard he was greeted by a red-haired man who immediately became friendly and enquired if Mr. Pickwick was going to Ipswich. On learning that he was, and that he, too, had taken an outside seat, they became fast friends. Little did Mr. Pickwick suppose that his newly made friend and he would meet again later under less congenial circumstances.

"Take care o' the archway, gen'l'men," was Sam's timely warning as the coach, under the control of his father, started out of the inn yard on its memorable journey down Whitechapel Road to the "Great White Horse," Ipswich, an hostelry which forms the subject of the following chapter.

Chapter X

THE "GREAT WHITE HORSE," IPSWICH
***

"In the main street of Ipswich, on the left-hand side of the way, a short distance after you have passed through the open space fronting the Town Hall, stands an inn known far and wide by the appellation of the 'Great White Horse,' rendered the more conspicuous by a stone statue of some rampacious animal with flowing mane and tail, distantly resembling an insane cart horse, which is elevated above the principal door."

With these identical words Dickens introduces his readers to, and indicates precisely, the position of the famous Great White Horse Inn at Ipswich, and a visitor to the popular city of Suffolk need have no better guide to the spot than the novelist. He will be a little surprised at the description of the white horse, which in reality is quite an unoffending and respectable animal, in the act of simply lifting its fore leg in a trotting action, that is all; but he will be well repaid if when he arrives there he reads again Chapter XXII of The Pickwick Papers before he starts to make himself acquainted with the intricacies of the interior.

That chapter, telling of the extraordinary adventure Mr. Pickwick experienced with the middle-aged lady in the double-bedded room, is one of the most amusing in the book, and one which has made the "Great White Horse" as familiar a name as any in fiction or reality.

There are few inns in the novelist's books described so fully. He must have known it well; indeed, he is supposed to have stayed there when, in his early days, he visited Ipswich to report an election for The Morning Chronicle; and probably a similar mistake happened to him to that which Mr. Pickwick experienced. So when he says, "The 'Great Horse' is famous in the neighbourhood, in the same degree as a prize ox, or county paper-chronicled turnip, or unwieldy pig – for its enormous size," he evidently was recalling an impression of those days.

It is an imposing structure viewed from without, with stuccoed walls, and a pillared entrance, over which stands the sign which so attracted the novelist's attention. The inside is spacious, with still the air of the old days about it, and contains fifty bedrooms and handsome suites of rooms; but Dickens was a little misleading regarding its size and a little unkind in his reproaches. At any rate, if the seemingly unkind things he said of it were deserved in those days of which he writes, they are no longer.

"Never were such labyrinths of uncarpeted passages," he says; "such clusters of mouldy, ill-lighted rooms, such huge numbers of small dens for eating or sleeping in, beneath any one roof, as are collected together between the four walls of the Great White Horse Inn."

Here on a certain very eventful day appeared Mr. Pickwick, who was to have met his friends there, but as they had not arrived when he and Mr. Peter Magnus reached it by coach, he accepted the latter's invitation to dine with him.

Dickens's disparaging descriptions of the inn's accommodation lead one to believe that his experiences of the "over-grown tavern," as he calls it, were not of the pleasantest. He refers to the waiter as a corpulent man with "a fortnight's napkin" under his arm, and "coeval stockings," and tells how this worthy ushered Mr. Pickwick and Mr. Magnus into "a large badly furnished apartment, with a dirty grate, in which a small fire was making a wretched attempt to be cheerful, but was fast sinking beneath the dispiriting influence of the place." Here they made their repast from a "bit of fish and a steak," and "having ordered a bottle of the most horrible port wine, at the highest possible price, for the good of the house, drank brandy and water for their own." After finishing their scanty meal they were conducted to their respective bedrooms, each with a japanned candlestick, through "a multitude of torturous windings." Mr. Pickwick's "was a tolerably large double-bedded room, with a fire;

upon the whole, a more comfortable looking apartment than Mr. Pickwick's short experience of the accommodation of the 'Great White Horse' had led him to expect."

Whether all this was ever true does not seem to have mattered much to the various proprietors, for they were not only proud of the association of the inn with Pickwick, but made no attempt to hide what the novelist said of its shortcomings. On the contrary, one of them printed in a little booklet the whole of the particular chapter wherein these disrespectful remarks appear. Indeed, that is the chief means of advertisement to lure the traveller in, and when he gets there he finds Pickwick pictures everywhere on the walls to dispel any doubt he might have of the associations.

It is not necessary to re-tell the story of Mr. Pickwick's misadventure here. It will be recalled that having forgotten his watch he, in a weak moment, walked quietly downstairs, with the japanned candlestick in his hand, to secure it again. "The more stairs Mr. Pickwick went down, the more stairs there seemed to be to descend, and again and again, when Mr. Pickwick got into some narrow passage, and began to congratulate himself on having gained the ground floor, did another flight of stairs appear before his astonished eyes. . . . Passage after passage did he explore; room after room did he peep into"; until at length he discovered the room he wanted and also his watch.

The same difficulty confronted him on his journey backward; indeed, it was even more perplexing. "Rows of doors, garnished with boots of every shape, make, and size, branched off in every possible direction." He tried a dozen doors before he found what he thought was his room and proceeded to divest himself of his clothes preparatory to entering on his night's rest. But, alas! he had got into the wrong bedroom and the story of the dilemma he shortly found himself in with the lady in the yellow curl-papers, and how he extricated himself in so modest and gentlemanly a manner, is a story which "every schoolboy knows."

Having disentangled himself from the dilemma, he found the intricacies of the "White Horse's" landings and stairs again too much for him, until he was discovered, crouching in a recess in the wall, by his faithful servant Sam, who conducted him to his right room. Here Mr. Pickwick made a wise resolve that if he were to stop in the "Great White Horse" for six months, he would never trust himself about in it alone again.

We do not suppose that the visitor would encounter the same difficulty to-day in getting about the house as did Mr. Pickwick; but torturous passages are there all the same; and by virtue of Mr. Pickwick's experiences they are perhaps more noticeable than would otherwise appear had not his adventures been given to the world. And so the fact remains that Mr. Pickwick's spirit seems to haunt the building, and no attempt is made to disabuse the mind that his escapade was anything but an amusing if unfortunate reality.

The double-bedded room is a double-bedded room still, with its old four-posters, and is shown with great pride to visitors from all over the world as "Mr. Pickwick's room." The beds are still hung with old-fashioned curtains, and a rush-bottomed chair has its place there, as it did during Mr. Pickwick's visit. Even the wall-paper is not of a modern pattern, and may have survived from that historic night. At least these things were the same when we last visited it.

Indeed, all the rooms have still the atmosphere of the Victorian era about them. The coffee-room, the bar-parlour, the dining-room, the courtyard and the assembly room reflect the Pickwickian period, which in other words speak of "home-life ease and comfort," and "are not subordinate to newfangled ideas." Whether the small room in the vicinity of the stable-yard, where Mr. Weller, senior, was engaged in preparing for his journey to London, taking sustenance, and incidentally discussing "Widders" with his son Sam, exists to-day we are unable to state with any certainty; but no doubt there is one which would fill the bill. Which, too, was the particular room where Mr. Pickwick and Mr. Tupman were arrested, the former on the charge of intending to fight a duel, and the latter as aider and abettor, history does not relate, or modern research reveal.

The inn is some four hundred years old, and at one time was known as the White Horse Tavern. George II is said to have stayed there some three hundred years ago, and so, report has it, did Nelson and Lady Hamilton; but these are small matters compared to the larger ones connected with Mr. Pickwick, and merit but passing record. Whilst those details concerning the fictitious character can be adjusted by any enthusiast who stays at the "Great White Horse" on a Pickwickian pilgrimage, no tangible trace that the three other historical personages used the inn remains to substantiate the fact, although the tradition is acceptable.

Chapter XI

THE "GEORGE AND VULTURE"
***

Tucked away in the heart of the busiest part of the roaring city, overshadowed by tall, hard-looking, modern banking and insurance buildings and all but a thin strip of it hidden from view, is a veritable piece of old London.

This is the "George and Vulture," known throughout the world as the tavern that Mr. Pickwick and his friends made their favourite city headquarters. The address in the directory of this inn is St. Michael's Alley, Cornhill; The Pickwick Papers, however, describe it as being in George Yard, Lombard Street. Both are correct. If the latter address is followed, the inn is not easy to find, for the sign "Old Pickwickian Hostel" is so high up over the upper window in the far left-hand corner that it is almost the last thing one sees. One fares little better from the other approach, for the narrow alley with its tall buildings facing each other so closely as to be almost touched with outstretched arms, makes it necessary to search for the entrance doorway.

These, however, are not drawbacks to the lover of old London, for he rather prefers to probe about for things he likes, particularly when, as in this case, the discovery is worth the trouble; for once inside the "George and Vulture" the pilgrim will be thoroughly recompensed for the trouble he has taken in finding it. Here he will be struck by the atmosphere of old time which still prevails, even though there are signs that the modern has somewhat supplanted the old. Not long since the dining-room on the ground floor was well sawdusted, and partitioned off in the old coffee-room style, and some of these high-backed box-like compartments still remain in corners of the room. With the knowledge that this ancient hostelry was called "Thomas's Chop House" – and it still bears that name ground on the glass doors – one expects to discover a grill loaded up with fizzing chops and steaks, and there it will be found, presided over by the white-garbed chef turning over the red-hot morsels.

Opposite the door is the old-fashioned bar, with a broad staircase winding up by its side to another dining-room above completely partitioned off into compartments with still another grill and a spotlessly robed chef in evidence. Up another flight of stairs we come to yet one more dining-room recently decorated in the old style, with oak-beamed ceiling and surroundings to match; with lantern lights suspended from the oak beams, grandfather clock, warming pan, pewter plates and odd pieces of furniture in keeping with the period it all seeks to recall. It is called the "Pickwick Room," and this metamorphosis was carried out by a city business firm for the accommodation of its staff at lunch, and its good friendship toward them admirably reflects the Dickens spirit. Here the members of the general staff, both ladies and gentlemen, numbering about 170, daily gather for their midday meal; whilst a small cosy room adjoining is et apart for the managerial heads. On occasions, representatives of associated houses in the city and from abroad, calling on business, are cordially invited to join the luncheon party.

There is an interesting Visitors' Book in the Pickwick Room, wherein guests are asked to inscribe their names and designations; also a private or business motto. Custom has it that a man only signs the book once, however many times he may visit the Pickwick Room, unless his official position has altered through business promotion.

This being the floor tradition has decided was Mr. Pickwick's bedroom, it is suitably decorated with Pickwickian and Dickensian pictures and ornaments, all tending to remind the visitor of the homely period of the past. There are no bedrooms to-day in the inn, nor are there any comfortable so-called sitting- or coffee-rooms, for all the available space is required for satisfying the hungry city man.

The history of the "George and Vulture" goes back some centuries. Originally it was the London lodging of Earl Ferrers, and in 1175 a brother of his was slain there in the night. It was then called simply the "George," and described by Stow, the great historian of London, as "a common hostelry for travellers."

Ultimately the "Vulture," for reasons undiscovered by the present writer, was added to the sign, and the appellation the "George and Vulture" has come through the history of London unaltered, gathering with the flight of time many famous associations to keep its memory green in each succeeding period, until Mr. Pickwick put the coping-stone to its fame as one of London's imperishable heritages.

Poets and literary men of all degrees frequented it from the earliest times, and although there is no record available to substantiate a claim that the great Chaucer used the house, it seems possible that his father, who was himself a licensed victualler in the district, knew it well. But John Skelton, the satirical poet of the fifteenth century, undoubtedly enjoyed its hospitality, for he has left record in the following lines that he was acquainted with it:

> Intent on signs, the prying eye,
> The George & Vulture will descry.
> Let none the outward Vulture fear,
> No Vulture host inhabits here.

> If too well used you deem ye then
> Take your revenge and come agen.

Taverns in those days were the resort of most of the prominent men of the day, and were used in the same manner by them as the clubs of the present time, as a friendly meeting place for business men, authors, artists, lawyers, doctors, actors and the fashionable persons of leisured ease with no particular calling, all of whom treated "mine host" as an equal and not as a servant.

And so we find that men like Addison and Steele were much in evidence at these friendly gatherings of their day; that Jonathan Swift and his coterie foregathered in some cosy corner to discuss the pros and cons of that great fraud, the South Sea Bubble; that Daniel Defoe was a constant guest of the host of his time; that John Wilkes and his fellow-members of "The Hell Fire Club" used the house for their meetings, and many others the recital of whose names would resolve into a mere catalogue.

In 1666 the inn succumbed to the Great Fire; but after the rebuilding its fame was re-established and has never since waned. John Strype, the ecclesiastical historian, in his addenda to Stow's Survey of London, records that "Near Ball Alley was the George Inn, since the fire rebuilt, with very good houses and warehouses, being a large open yard, and called

George Yard, at the farther end of which is the 'George and Vulture' Tavern, which is a large house and having great trade, and having a passage into St. Michael's Alley."

The yard referred to is now filled with large buildings, but when it existed as part of the inn was used, like other inn yards, by the travelling companies of players for the enactment of their mystery and morality plays. It was in the "George and Vulture," so it is recorded, that the first Beefsteak Club was formed by Richard Estcourt, the Drury Lane comedian, a fashion which spread in all directions. And so the history of the "George and Vulture" could be traced, and anecdotes relating to it set down to fill many pages. But whilst admitting that these antiquarian notes have their interest for their own sake, we must leave them in order that we may glance at the Pickwickian traditions, through which the tavern is known to-day.

In our last chapter we left Mr. Pickwick at the "Great White Horse," Ipswich. On his return to London he had, perforce, to abandon his lodgings in Goswell Street and so transferred his abode to very good old-fashioned and comfortable quarters, to wit, the George and Vulture Tavern and Hotel, George Yard, Lombard Street, and forthwith sent Sam to settle the little matters of rent and such-like trifles and to bring back his little odds and ends from Goswell Street. This done they shortly left the tavern for Dingley Dell, where they had a royal Christmas time. That the tavern appealed to Mr. Pickwick as ideal for the entertainment of friends is incidentally revealed in the record that after one of the merry evenings at Mr. Wardle's he, on waking late next morning, had "a confused recollection of having severally and confidentially invited somewhere about five and forty people to dine with him at the 'George and Vulture' the very first time they came to London."

Just before they left Dingley Dell, Bob Sawyer, "thrusting his forefinger between two of Mr. Pickwick's ribs and thereby displaying his native drollery and his knowledge of the anatomy of the human frame at one and the same time, enquired – 'I say, old boy, where do you hang out?' Mr. Pickwick replied that he was at present suspended at the 'George and Vulture'!"

Whether Mr. Pickwick had some idea of finding other quarters when he said he was "at present suspended" we do not know; at all events he made the tavern his London residence until, at the end of his adventures, he retired to Dulwich. Before, however, he settled down there, many incidents connected with his career took place within the walls of his favourite tavern. It was in his sitting-room here that the subpoenas re Bardell v. Pickwick were served on his three friends and Sam Weller on behalf of the plaintiff. The Pickwickians were seated round the fire after a comfortable dinner when Mr. Jackson, the plaintiff's man, by his unexpected appearance, disturbed their happy gathering. It was from the "George and Vulture" they all drove to the Guildhall on the day of the trial, and it was in Mr. Pickwick's room in the tavern that he vowed to Mr. Perker he would never pay even a halfpenny of the damages.

The next morning the Pickwickians again continued their travels, Bath being their choice of place. Returning after a week's absence, we are told that Mr. Pickwick with Sam "straightway returned to his old quarters at the 'George and Vulture.'" Before another week elapsed the fateful and inevitable day came when Mr. Pickwick was arrested and eventually conveyed to the Fleet Prison. He was in bed at the time, and so annoyed was Sam that he threatened to pitch the officer of the law out of the window into the yard below. Mr. Pickwick's deliverance from prison took him once again to the "George and Vulture," and to him came Arabella Allan and Winkle to announce to him that they were man and wife and made it their place of residence whilst Mr. Pickwick went off to Birmingham to make peace with Nathaniel's father. Mr. Winkle, senior, eventually visited the old hostel and formally approved of his daughter-in-law.

It was whilst in the inn also that Sam Weller received the news of the death of his "mother-in-law," conveyed in the extraordinary letter from his father, which he read to Mary in one of the window seats.

Here, also, came Tony Weller to make his offer of the L530 "reduced counsels" which he had inherited, to Mr. Pickwick, adding – "P'raps it'll go a little way towards the expenses o' that 'ere conwiction. All I say is, just you keep it till I ask you for it again," and bolted out of the room.

The last specific reference to the "George and Vulture" is on the occasion when the party left it to join Mr. Wardle and other friends at dinner at Osborne's Adelphi Hotel. So, it will be seen, from the first mention of the tavern about midway through the book, until its closing pages, the "George and Vulture" may be said to have been Mr. Pickwick's headquarters in London.

Is it, therefore, to be wondered at, considering all the incidents and events these few references recall, that the whole atmosphere of the "George and Vulture" positively reeks with Pickwick?

Is it surprising that the various proprietors of the inn have from time to time cherished these associations, and none more so than the present genial proprietor and his efficient manager, Mr. Woods, and have reminded their customers each time they dine there of Mr. Pickwick's connection with it by placing before them plates with that immortal man's portrait in the act of addressing his club, printed thereon?

Is it to be wondered at that the City Pickwick Club should hold its meetings and dinners there, or that the Dickens Fellowship should choose it as the most appropriate spot for the entertainment of their American and colonial visitors, and occasionally to have convivial gatherings of its members there?

And will it surprise anyone if a universal agitation is set on foot to preserve it from the axe and pick of the builder which threatens it in the near future?

There is one extraordinarily interesting piece of history relative to the "George and Vulture" and Pickwick with which fittingly to close this account of London's famous inn.

In 1837, the year that The Pickwick Papers appeared in monthly-parts, a Circulating Book Society had its headquarters at the "George and Vulture." On the occasion of the meeting held on March 30, 1837, it was proposed that The Pickwick Papers, "now in course of publication, be taken in for circulation."

This motion was opposed by two members "who considered the work vulgar." The motion, however, was carried with the amendment "that the work, when complete, be obtained and circulated as one volume." In 1838 this famous copy of the immortal work was sold by auction amongst the members, in what was probably the very room Dickens had in mind when describing the meetings of Mr. Pickwick and his friends. It was bought by J. Buckham for 13s. 6d. This copy was annotated by the owner with notes, historical and explanatory, and is now a cherished possession of the nation in the safe custody of the Library of the British Museum, where it is known as the "George and Vulture" copy.

Chapter XII

THE "BLUE BOAR, "LEADENHALL MARKET," GARRAWAY'S," AND THE "WHITE HORSE CELLAR"
***

The "Blue Boar," Leadenhall Market, was an inn of considerable Pickwickian importance. It was the elder Weller's favourite house of call, and it will be remembered that Sam was sent for by his father on one occasion to meet him there at six o'clock. Having obtained Mr. Pickwick's permission to absent himself from the "George and Vulture," Sam sauntered down as far as the Mansion House, and then by easy stages wended his way towards Leadenhall Market, through a variety of by-streets and courts, purchasing a Valentine on his way.

Looking round him he beheld a signboard on which the painter's art had delineated something remotely resembling a cerulean elephant with an aquiline nose in lieu of a trunk. Rightly conjecturing that this was the "Blue Boar" himself, he stepped into the house and enquired concerning his parent. Finding that his father would not be there for three-quarters of an hour or more, he ordered from the barmaid "nine penn'orth o' brandy and water hike, and the inkstand," and having settled himself in the little parlour, composed himself to write that wonderful "walentine" to Mary. Just as Sam had finished his missive his father appeared on the scene, and he was invited by the dutiful son to listen to what he had written. Tony heard it through, punctuating it during the process with a running commentary and much advice on marriage in general and "widders" in particular.

It was here, too, that Tony, with the laudable intention of helping Mr. Pickwick, offered the invaluable, and now historic, advice concerning an "alleybi," there being, as he asserted, "nothing like a' alleybi, Sammy, nothing."

It was in the same parlour on the same occasion that Mr. Weller, senior, informed his son that he had two tickets "as wos sent" to Mrs. Weller by the Shepherd "for the monthly meetin' o' the Brick Lane Branch o' the United Grand Junction Ebenezer Temperance Association." He communicated the secret "with great glee and winked so indefatigably after doing so," "over a double glass o' the inwariable," that he and Sam determined to make use of the tickets with the projected plan of exposing the "real propensities and qualities of the red-nosed man," the success of which is so well remembered.

These facts in mind the "Blue Boar" ought not to be passed over lightly, even though it cannot be identified by name, or its existence traced in historic records. In those days the description of the locality given by

Dickens was accurate enough; but although there were many inns and taverns in its district, topographers have never discovered a "Blue Boar," or learned that one ever bore such a sign. There was a "Bull" in Leadenhall Street at one time, and possibly this may have been the inn the novelist made the scene of the above incidents, simply giving it a name of his own to afford scope for his whimsical vein in describing it.

However, the locality has changed completely from what it was when Tony Weller "used the parlour" of the "Blue Boar," and such coaching inns that flourished then have all been swept away with the "shabby courts and alleys."

We find, however, a picture purporting to be the "Blue Boar" with its galleries, horses and stable boys all complete drawn by Herbert Railton, in the Jubilee edition of The Pickwick Papers. Probably this is purely an imaginary picture.

On the other hand, there was nothing visionary about Garraway's. "Garraway's, twelve o'clock. 'Dear Mrs. B., Chops and Tomato Sauce, Yours, Pickwick,'" not only implicated Mr. Pickwick, but conjured up an old and historic coffee house of city fame. It stood in Exchange Alley, and was a noted meeting-place for city men, and for its sales and auctions. It was demolished some fifty years ago after an existence of over two hundred years. It claimed to be the first to sell tea "according to the directions of the most knowing merchants and travellers into the eastern countries," but ultimately became more famous for its sandwiches and sherry. No doubt it was the latter, or something even more substantial, that Mr. Pickwick had been indulging during the day he wrote that momentous message. Garraway's was known to Defoe, Dean Swift, Steele and others, each of whom have references to it in their books, and during its affluent days it was never excelled by other taverns in the city for good fare and comfort. It was there that the "South Sea Bubblers" frequently met.

Garraway's is mentioned in other books of Dickens. In Martin Chuzzlewit, for instance, Nadgett, who undertook the task of making secret enquiries for the Anglo-Bengalee business, used to sit in Garraway's, and was occasionally seen drying a damp pocket handkerchief before the fire, looking over his shoulder for the man who never appeared.

It is also referred to in Little Dorrit as one of the coffee houses frequented by Mr. Flintwich.

In The Uncommercial Traveller, in writing about the "City of the Absent," Dickens makes this further allusion to the tavern:

"There is an old monastery-cript under Garraway's (I have been in it among the port wine), and perhaps

Garraway's, taking pity on the mouldy men who wait in its public room, all their lives, gives them cool house-room down there on Sundays."

Again in Christmas Stories the narrator of the "Poor Relation's Story" who lived in a lodging in the Clapham Road, tells how, amongst other things, he used to sit in Garraway's Coffee House in the city to pass away the time until it was time to dine, afterwards returning to his lodgings in the evening.

But of all these references, Mr. Pickwick's mention of Garraway's in his note to Mrs. Bardell is the one which will prevent its name and fame from being forgotten more than any other incident connected with it that we know of.

The "White Horse Cellar" from which the Pickwickians set out on the coach journey to Bath stood, at the time, at the corner of Arlington Street, Piccadilly, on the site occupied by the "Ritz" to-day. It was as famous and notorious as any coaching office in London; perhaps being in close proximity to the park and being in the west end, more famous than any.

In those flourishing days of its existence it was the starting-point of all the mails for the west of England, and was a bustling centre of activity. It was, apparently, one of the "sights" of London, for on fine evenings those with leisure on their hands would gather to watch the departure of these coaches. The scene became more like a miniature fair, with itinerants selling oranges, pencils, sponges and such-like commodities, to the passengers and the spectators.

Mr. Pickwick chose to take an early morning coach, perhaps to avoid the sightseers. In his anxiety he arrived much too soon and had to take shelter in the travellers' room – the last resort, as Dickens assures us, of human dejection.

"The travellers' room at the 'White Horse Cellar' is, of course, uncomfortable," he writes; "it would be no travellers' room if it were not. It is the right-hand parlour, into which an aspiring kitchen fire-place appears to have walked, accompanied by a rebellious poker, tongs and shovel. It is divided into boxes for the solitary confinement of travellers, and is furnished with a clock, a looking-glass, and a live waiter, which latter article is kept in a small kennel for washing glasses in a corner of the apartment."

Whilst taking his breakfast therein, Mr. Pickwick made the acquaintance of Mr. and Mrs. Dowler, also bound for Bath, who were to play such an unexpected part in his sojourn in the famous watering-place.

It was outside the "White Horse Cellar" that Sam Weller made that discovery about the use of Mr.

Pickwick's name which so annoyed him. Whilst the party were mounting the coach he observed that the proprietor's name, written in bold letters on the coach, was no other than "Pickwick." He drew his master's attention to it, but Mr. Pickwick merely thought it a very extraordinary thing. Sam, on the other hand, was of the opinion that the "properiator" was playing some "imperence" with them. "Not content," he said, "vith writin' up Pickwick, they puts 'Moses' afore it, vich I call addin' insult to injury, as the parrot said ven they not only took him from his native land, but made him talk the English langvidge arterwards."

The "White Horse Cellar" ultimately was moved to the opposite side of Piccadilly, and in 1884, the new "White Horse" in turn was pulled down, upon whose site was erected the "Albemarle."

The "White Horse Cellar" is also mentioned in Bleak House in the communication from Kenge and Carboys to Esther Summerson as her halting-place in London. Here she was met by their clerk, Mr. Guppy, who later, in his declaration of love to her, reminded her of his services on that occasion – "I think you must have seen that I was struck with those charms on the day when I waited at the whytorseller. I think you must have remarked that I could not forbear a tribute to those charms when I put up the steps of the 'ackney coach."

Chapter XIII

FOUR BATH INNS AND THE "BUSH," BRISTOL
***

On their arrival at Bath, Mr. Pickwick and his friends and Mr. Dowler and his wife "respectively retired to their private sitting-rooms at the White Hart Hotel, opposite the great Pump Room . . . where waiters, from their costume, might be mistaken for Westminster boys, only they destroyed the illusion by behaving themselves so much better."

Mr. Pickwick had scarcely finished his breakfast next morning when Mr. Dowler brought in no less a person than his friend, Angelo Cyrus Bantam, Esquire, to introduce to him, and to administer his stock greeting, "Welcome to Ba-ath, sir. This is, indeed, an acquisition. Most welcome to Ba-ath, sir."

For the story of the various adventures which overtook the Pickwickians in the famous city, what they saw, and what they did, the reader must be referred to the official chronicle, except where they are connected with some inn or tavern.

So far as the "White Hart" is concerned, there is little to be said in this direction. After the reception at the Assembly Rooms on the evening after their arrival,

Mr. Pickwick accompanied his friends back to the "White Hart," and "having soothed his feelings with something hot, went to bed, and to sleep, almost simultaneously."

As Mr. Pickwick contemplated staying in Bath for at least two months, he deemed it advisable to take lodgings for himself and his friends for that period. This he did, and the "White Hart" has no further association with his person during his stay in the gay city.

The "White Hart," nevertheless, has a very strong claim to Pickwickian fame, apart from the brief fact that the founder of the club stayed there a night or two. At the time, the "White Hart" belonged to the very Moses Pickwick whose name on the coach so worried poor Sam Weller at the start of their journey down from London.

This Moses Pickwick was a grandson of Eleazer Pickwick, who, it is recorded, was a foundling. The story told concerning him is that when an infant he was picked up by a lady in the village of Wick near Bath, carried to her home, adopted and educated. Hence, according to some, the name Pick-Wick. There is, however, a village near to hand actually called "Pickwick," which may also have inspired the name for the foundling.

For some reasons unknown, or, at any rate, unrevealed, this foundling developed a craze for the coaching business, and, ultimately, taking service in one of the coaching inns, devoted his time and interests whole-heartedly to the profession, or calling. Eventually he became the owner of the business.

His grandson, Moses, became even more famous during the coaching era than his foundling antecedent, and at the time Pickwick was written he was the actual proprietor of the White Hart Hotel, as well as of the coaches which ran to and from it. He became, also, the most popular owner in the trade, and retired to the village of Upper Swanswick a rich man. We believe the name is still perpetuated in the neighbourhood.

Now it is known as a fact that Dickens took the name Pickwick from the said Moses Pickwick the proprietor of the "White Hart," whose coaches he had seen and ridden in a year or two previously. So that apart from the brief references to the inn in The Pickwick Papers its history is very much associated with the book.

Unfortunately, Dickens does not give us any minute description of it, as he does of other inns. Although it was the most important coaching house in the city, it could not be spoken of as particularly attractive in appearance. It looked more like a barracks than an hotel, indeed, we believe it was used for such a purpose in its degenerate days before it was finally demolished in 1867.

During its prosperous era, it was the resort of all the distinguished visitors who flocked to Bath during those gay and festive times.

There is still a relic of it in existence. The gracefully carved effigy of a white hart, which decorated the front of the building, now serves a similar purpose on an inn with the same name in the suburb of Widcombe, near by. On the site of the old house now stands the Grand Pump Room Hotel.

The Royal Hotel to which Mr. Winkle resorted, after his adventure with the valorous Dowler, for the purpose of escape to Bristol by the branch coach, probably never existed – at any rate, by that name. Dickens may have had the "York House" in his mind, for he stayed there himself on one occasion, and it was one of those ornate hotels, accustomed to receiving royal and distinguished visitors, suggesting such a title as Dickens gave it.

There is, however, a tavern in Bath which claimed – or was made to claim – a Pickwickian association, and that is the Beaufort Arms. The story in connection with it is that before it was a tavern it was originally "the small greengrocer's shop" over which the Bath footmen held their social evenings, and was, therefore, the scene of the memorable "leg o' mutton swarry," given in honour of Sam Weller. This may be so; we prefer to think that it was more likely to have been the public-house from which, as we are told, drinks were fetched for that dignified function.

The "Saracen's Head" in the same city has a Dickensian, if not a Pickwickian, interest, for Dickens stayed there when, in his journalistic days, he was following Lord John Russell through the country in 1835, reporting his speeches. We can be sure that it was during this brief visit that he gained an insight into the social doings and customs of the city, and also gathered the extensive knowledge of its topography his book exhibits. The "Saracen's Head" is proud of its Dickens associations; the actual chair he sat in, the actual jug he drank from, and the actual room he slept in are each shown with much ado to visitors; whilst several anecdotes associated with the novelist's visit on the occasion are re-told with perfect assurance of their truth.

Arriving at Bristol after his flight from Mr. Dowler at Bath, Mr. Winkle took up his quarters at the "Bush," there only to encounter later in the day "the figure of the vindictive and sanguinary Dowler" himself. Explanations soon smoothed over their little differences, and they parted for the night "with many protestations of eternal friendship."

In the meantime, Sam Weller had been sent posthaste on Mr. Winkle's heels with instructions from Mr. Pickwick to lock him in his bedroom as soon as he found him. Sam was nothing loath, and when he had run Winkle to earth at the "Bush", promptly carried out his master's orders and awaited his further instructions as to what to do next. These were brought next morning by Mr. Pickwick, in person, when he walked into the coffee-loom. Satisfaction being arrived at, the three stayed on at the "Bush" for a day or two, experiencing some curious adventures in the neighbourhood during the time.

On another occasion Mr. Pickwick and Sam stayed at the "Bush," and after dinner the former adjourned to the travellers' room, where, Sam informed him, "there was only a gentleman with one eye, and the landlord, who were drinking a bowl of bishop together."

"He's a queer customer, the vun-eyed vun, sir," observed Mr. Weller, as he led the way. "He's a-gammonin' that 'ere landlord, he is, sir, till he don't rightly know vether he's standing on the soles of his boots or on the crown of his hat."

This was no other than the man who told the story of Tom Smart at the "Peacock," Eatanswill, and he was ready and willing to tell another; with little persuasion he settled down and related the story of the Bagman's Uncle.

The "Bush" was, in its time, the chief coaching inn of the city, and one of the headquarters of Moses Pickwick's coaching business. It stood until 1864, near the Guildhall, and its site is now occupied by Lloyd's Bank. This was another inn that Dickens stayed at in 1835 whilst reporting for The Morning Chronicle. Writing from that address he says he expects to forward the conclusion of Russell's dinner "by Cooper's company coach, leaving the 'Bush' at half-past six next morning; and by the first Bell's coach on Thursday he will forward the report of the Bath dinner, endorsing the parcel for immediate delivery with extra rewards for the porter."

Chapter XIV

THE "FOX UNDER THE HILL," OTHER LONDON TAVERNS, AND THE "SPANIARDS," HAMPSTEAD
***

On his return from Bath, Mr. Pickwick was immediately arrested and conveyed to the Fleet Prison. In the course of the chapters following this event there are several inns or taverns either mentioned incidentally, or figure more or less prominently, such as the new public-house opposite the Fleet, the "Fox Under the Hill," Sarjeants' Inn Coffee House, the public-house, opposite the Insolvent Debtors' Court, the Horn Coffee House in the Doctors' Commons and the "Spaniards," Hampstead Heath. Of these the "Fox Under the Hill," casually referred to by Mr. Roker as the spot where Tom Martin "whopped the coach-heaver," was situated on the Thames water-side in the Adelphi, at the bottom of Ivy Lane. The incident he related was no doubt a recollection of Dickens's early days in the blacking factory at Hungerford Stairs, for the public-house was known to him, as the following sentence in his biography shows – "One of his favourite realities was a little public-house by the water-side called the 'Fox Under the Hill,' approached by an underground passage which we once missed on looking for it together"; and he had a vision which he has mentioned in Copperfield of sitting eating something on a bench outside, one fine evening, and looking at some coal-heavers dancing before the house.

The public-house, nevertheless, was there when Dickens and his biographer were seeking it, for it was not demolished until the Victoria Embankment was built many years later.

Robert Allbut states that the "Fox Under the Hill" was the tavern where Martin Chuzzlewit, junior, was accommodated when he arrived in London, and where he was visited by Mark Tapley.

The public-house opposite the Insolvent Debtors' Court, where Mr. Weller consulted Mr. Solomon Pell on an urgent family matter, was no doubt the "Horse and Groom" that once stood in Portugal Street, covered now by the solid buildings of Messrs. W. H. Smith and Sons, of railway bookstall fame. It was here Sam obliged the company with his song on "Bold Turpin," whilst his father and Solomon Pell went to swear the affidavit for Sam's arrest. It was also at this identical public-house that Mr. Solomon Pell, later on in the book, was engaged to undertake the details of proving the Will of the late Mrs. Weller, and where, "to celebrate Mr. Weller coming into possession of his property," a little lunch was given to his friends, comprising porter, cold beef and oysters, to which ample justice was done.

Reverting to the former incident, the elder Weller and Solomon Pell duly returned with the document all complete, and the party sallied forth to the Fleet Prison. On their way they stopped at Sarjeants' Inn Coffee House off Fleet Street to refresh themselves once more. When Sarjeants' Inn was rebuilt in 1838 the coffee house referred to ended its existence.

The Horn Coffee House in Doctors' Commons, to which a messenger was despatched from the Fleet Prison for "a bottle or two of very good wine" to celebrate Mr. Winkle's visit to his old friend, was a well-known and frequented place of call at the time. It was situated actually in Carter Lane, and although the present house is more in keeping with modern methods, there still remains a portion of the old building.

The "Spaniards," Hampstead Heath, figures more prominently in the book than any of the foregoing, and has a story of its own to tell. In recalling the scene in its history which associates it with The Pickwick Papers, we remember that Mrs. Bardell and her friends, Mrs. Sanders, Mrs. Cluppins, Mr. and Mrs. Raddle, Mrs. Rogers and Master Tommy Bardell, bent on having a day out, had taken the Hampstead Stage to the "Spaniards" Tea Gardens, "where the luckless Mr. Raddle's very first act nearly occasioned his good lady a relapse, it being neither more or less than to order tea for seven;

whereas (as the ladies one and all remarked) what could have been easier than for Tommy to have drank out of any lady's cup, or everybody's, if that was all, when the waiter wasn't looking, which would have saved one head of tea, and the tea just as good!"

But the brilliant suggestion was made too late, for "the tea-tray came with seven cups and saucers, and bread and butter on the same scale. Mrs. Bardell was unanimously voted into the chair, and Mrs. Rogers being stationed on her right hand and Mrs. Raddle on her left, the meal proceeded with great merriment and success," until Mr. Raddle again put his foot into it by making an unfortunate remark which upset Mrs. Bardell and caused him to be summarily sent to a table by himself to finish his tea alone.

Mrs. Bardell had just recovered from her fainting fit when the ladies observed a hackney coach stop at the garden gate. Out of it stepped Mr. Jackson of Dodson and Fogg, who, coming up to the party, informed Mrs. Bardell that his "people" required her presence in the city directly on very important and pressing business. "How very strange," said Mrs. Bardell, with an air of being someone of distinction, as she allowed herself to be taken along, accompanied by Mrs. Sanders, Mrs. Cluppins and Tommy. Entering the coach in waiting, to be driven, as they thought, to Dodson and Fogg's, they were alas! sadly deceived, for shortly afterwards Mrs. Bardell was safely deposited in the Fleet Prison for not having paid those rascals their costs, and promptly fainted in "real downright earnest."

What happened to the rest of the party at the "Spaniards" history does not relate. But the event which had promised to be such a happy one at the famous old inn was spoiled by those rapscallions of lawyers, and we can only hope that Mr. Raddle made himself amiable with the two ladies left in his charge, and helped them to enjoy the remainder of the day in the pleasant rural and rustic spot.

The "Spaniards" is still a favourite resort of the pleasure-seeking pedestrian, and a halting-place for refreshment for pilgrims across the Heath. The arbours and rustic corners of its pleasant tea gardens still attract holiday-makers, as they attracted Mrs. Bardell and her friends on that day long since gone by.

The inn itself is spacious and offers the comforts expected of an ancient hostelry. Dating back to about 1630 it occupies what was once the lodge entrance to the Bishop of London's great rural park, whose old toll gate is still remaining. It is said by some to have derived its name through having been once inhabited by a family connected with the Spanish Embassy; and by others from its having been taken by a Spaniard who converted it into a house of refreshment and entertainment. Ultimately its gardens were improved and beautifully ornamented by one William Staples, similar to the gardens which flourished during this period in other parts of the metropolis. It has carried on its business of catering for all and sundry to the present day, but the ornate decorations and statuary have long disappeared.

The "Spaniards" is a Dick Turpin house, for, according to tradition, in its precincts the famous highwayman often hid from his pursuers. We are assured that in the out-house he found his favourite resting-place, which many a time on the late return of the marauder had served as his bedroom. The under-ground passages that led to the inn itself have been filled up, years ago. There were two doors attacked by unpleasant visitors, and a secret trap-door through which Turpin dived into the underground apartment, there to await the departure of the raging officers, or to betake himself to the inn, if that were clear of attack.

To such a fine Londoner as Dickens, who must have known it and his history thoroughly, it is a little surprising that it does not figure more prominently in his writings than it does. There is, indeed, one occasion when, it seems to us, he missed the opportunity of making it a picturesque and typical setting for a scene which his pen was more peculiarly suited than any other we know.

In Barndby Rudge he gives us vivid pen pictures of the Gordon Rioters setting fire to houses in London, prominent amongst them being that of Lord Mansfield, and goes on to describe how they proceeded to the country seat of the great Chief Justice at Caen Wood, Hampstead, to treat it in a similar fashion. On arriving there the rioters were met by the military, stopped in their nefarious deed, turned tail and returned to London – all in accordance with the historical facts which it is well known the novelist gathered from an authoritative document. But he does not tell us how the rioters were thwarted in their contemplated act, due, so runs the story, to the foresight of the landlord of the "Spaniards."

On their way to Lord Mansfield's house the rioters had to pass the Spaniards Inn, and the landlord, having been made aware of their approach and mission, stood at his door to meet them and enticed them in to drink whilst he sent a messenger to the barracks for a detachment of Horse Guards. In the interim his cellars were thrown open to the excited rebels, hot with irresponsibility from the devastation they had already made in London. Here he left them to themselves surrounded by all they might require to slake their thirsty appetites. By the time they had appeased this thirst and were ready to continue their journey to Lord Mansfield's house a few yards off, they discovered to their chagrin that their way was blocked by the arrival of a contingent of soldiers. And so in their wisdom they retraced their steps, as Dickens tells us, faster than they went.

Now the reason for this quick decision on the part of the rebels is passed over by Dickens, and the "Spaniards" is, in consequence, robbed of additional reflected glory, whilst the landlord is deprived of his place of immortality in the pages of Dickens's book, the one book on the "No Popery" riots that counts to-day. He does not even mention the Spaniards Inn in Barnaby Rudge, although the rioters are, in its pages, brought to the inn door, from which point they are turned back, and the famous seat of Lord Mansfield remains, if tradition be reliable, thanks to the landlord of the inn.

Chapter XV

THE "BELL," BERKELEY HEATH, THE "HOP POLE," TEWKESBURY, AND THE "OLD ROYAL," BIRMINGHAM
***

The chapter describing the Pickwickians' journey from the "Bush" Bristol to Birmingham, supplies incidents at four inns mentioned by name, and one that is not. The party comprising Mr. Pickwick and Mr. Benjamin Allen, Bob Sawyer and Sam Weller, sallied forth in a post-chaise. The two former seated themselves comfortably inside, whilst Bob Sawyer occupied a seat on the trunk on the top, and Sam settled himself in the dickey.

The two last-named were bent on making a merry day of it, and as soon as they were beyond the boundaries of Bristol they began their tricks by changing hats, taking liquid and substantial refreshments to the amusement of the passers-by, and the astonishment of Mr. Pickwick. But the journey need not be described here. Suffice it to say that the hilarious pair outside, come what may, meant to make a day of it. Their first stop, ostensibly to change horses, was at the "Bell," Berkeley Heath, on the high road between Bristol and Gloucester.

"I say, we're going to dine here, aren't we?" said Bob, looking in at the window.

"Dine!" said Mr. Pickwick. "Why, we have only come nineteen miles, and have got eighty-seven and a half to go."

"Just the reason why we should take something to enable us to bear up against the fatigue," remonstrated Mr. Bob Sawyer.

"Oh, it's quite impossible to dine at half-past eleven o'clock in the day," replied Mr. Pickwick, looking at his watch.

"So it is," rejoined Bob, "lunch is the very thing. Hallo, you sir! Lunch for three, directly, and keep the horses back for a quarter of an hour. Tell them to put everything they have cold, on the table, and some bottled ale, and let us taste your very best Madeira." Issuing these orders with monstrous importance and bustle, Mr. Bob Sawyer at once hurried into the house to superintend the arrangements; in less than five minutes he returned and declared them to be excellent.

The quality of the lunch fully justified the eulogium which Bob had pronounced, and very great justice was done to it, not only by that gentleman, but by Mr. Ben Allen and Mr. Pickwick also. In the hands of the thirsty three, the bottled ale and the Madeira were promptly disposed of; and when (the horses being once more put to) they resumed their seats, with the case-bottle full of the best substitute for milk-punch that could be procured on so short a notice, the key-bugle sounded, and the red flag waved, without the sightest opposition on Mr. Pickwick's part.

The unpretentious roadside inn still exists to-day, unaltered since the above-mentioned memorable occasion. It cherishes its Dickensian association by curiously and oddly announcing on its signboard that:

"Charles Dickens and Party lunched here 1827. B. C. Hooper."

It is within a mile of Berkeley Road Station on the Bristol Road, and about the same distance from the town of Berkeley. It lies back from the main road, and is a rambling old house and of good age. Although it has no more mention in the book than that given above, it is well known far and wide, nevertheless. As the Pickwickians did not stay there the inn is deprived of the privilege of showing a room in which the illustrious men slept, as is done in the case of other inns; but it has been recorded by one proprietor that travellers have called there for no other purpose than that of drinking Dickens's health in the snug parlour.

Continuing their journey the animated party reached in course of time the "Hop Pole" at Tewkesbury, where they stopped to dine; upon which occasion, we are assured, there was more bottled ale, with some more Madeira, and some port besides; and here the case-bottle was replenished for the fourth time. Under the influence of these combined stimulants, Mr. Pickwick and Mr. Ben Allen fell fast asleep for thirty miles, while Bob Sawyer and Sam Weller sang duets in the dickey.

The "Hop Pole" is still a flourishing country inn with the old-world flavour and atmosphere still clinging to it, where one is treated with the courtesy and welcome reminiscent of the old-time coaching days. Some modern "improvements" have been made in it, but its general appearance has not been tampered with, and it remains a veritable Dickens landmark of the town which the Tewkesbury Dickensians are proud of possessing. It is practically as it was in Pickwickian days, and the fact that Mr. Pickwick dined there is boldly announced at the side of the entrance, the porch of which did not however exist in those days.

From the "Hop Pole," Tewkesbury, the lively quartette continued their journey to Birmingham in a high-spirited mood and reached that city after dark.

"The postboy was driving briskly through the open streets and past the handsome and well-lighted shops which intervene between the outskirts of the town and the Royal Hotel, before Mr. Pickwick had begun to consider the very difficult and delicate nature of the commission which had carried him thither."

The difficulty and delicacy mentioned referred to the presence of Bob Sawyer and Ben Allen, whom Mr. Pickwick for certain reasons wished miles away, but he hoped to surmount them by making his interview with Mr. Winkle, senior, as brief as possible.

As he comforted himself with these reflections the chaise stopped at the door of the "Old Royal," and the visitors were shown to comfortable apartments. Mr. Pickwick immediately made enquiries of the waiter concerning the whereabouts of Mr. Winkle's residence, who was one not easily to be got the better of, as the following dialogue will show:

"'Close by, sir,' said the waiter, 'not above five hundred yards, sir. Mr. Winkle is a wharfinger, sir, at the canal, sir. Private residence is not – oh dear no, sir, not five hundred yards, sir.' Here the waiter blew a candle out and made a feint of lighting it again, in order to afford Mr. Pickwick an opportunity of asking any further questions, if he felt so disposed.

"'Take anything now, sir?' said the waiter, lighting the candle in desperation at Mr. Pickwick's silence. 'Tea or coffee, sir? Dinner, sir?'

"'Nothing now.'

"'Very good, sir. Like to order supper, sir?'

"'Not just now.'

"'Very good, sir.' Here he walked softly to the door, and then stopping short, turned round and said with great suavity:

"'Shall I send the chambermaid, gentlemen?'

"'You may if you please,' replied Mr. Pickwick.

"'If you please, sir.'

"'Bring some soda water,' said Bob Sawyer.

"'Soda water, sir? Yes, sir.' And with his mind apparently relieved from an overwhelming weight by having at last got an order for something, the waiter imperceptibly melted away. Waiters never walk or run. They have a peculiar and mysterious power of skimming out of rooms, which other mortals possess not."

Eventually Mr. Pickwick and his friends arrived safely at the house of Mr. Winkle, and, having concluded the interview, all three returned to the hotel and went "silent and supperless to bed."

The next day was a dreary and wet one, and, in contemplating the aspect from his bedroom window, Mr. Pickwick was attracted by a game cock in the stable yard, who, "deprived of every spark of his accustomed animation, balanced himself dismally on one leg in a corner." Then Mr. Pickwick discovered "a donkey, moping with drooping head under the narrow roof of an outhouse, who appeared from his meditative and miserable countenance to be contemplating suicide." In the breakfast-room there was very little conversation; even Mr. Bob Sawyer "felt the influence of the weather and the previous day's excitement, and in his own expressive language, he was 'floored.' So was Mr. Ben Allen. So was Mr. Pickwick."

The Pickwickians' visit, therefore, to the Royal Hotel was not a very bright and lively one, but they endeavoured to make the best of it.

"In protracted expectation of the weather clearing up, the last evening paper from London was read and re-read with an intensity of interest only known in cases of extreme destitution; every inch of the carpet was walked over with similar perseverance, the windows were looked out of often enough to justify the imposition of an additional duty upon them, all kinds of topics of conversation were started, and failed; and at length Mr. Pickwick, when noon had arrived without a change for the better, rang the bell resolutely and ordered out the chaise."

And so they started on their journey back in spite of the miserable 'outlook, feeling it was "infinitely superior to being pent in a dull room, looking at dull rain dripping into a dull street."

But Mr. Pickwick's lack of enthusiasm over the hotel was not due to the hotel itself, but more on account of the weather. As a fact, it was a very important hotel in those days. Attached to it were large assembly and concert rooms, erected in 1772 by Tontine. It was known as THE Hotel, the distinctive appellation of "Royal" being prefixed in consequence of a visit of a member of the royal family who took up his residence there for a time.

This is the only occasion the hotel has mention in the works of Dickens, and although Mr. Pickwick and his friends had no reason for being pleased with their visit to Birmingham's old inn, the reverse can be said of Dickens himself, for on more than one occasion he had pleasant associations of his stay there. The hotel has been rebuilt, but the picture shows it as it was in Mr. Pickwick's day.

Dickens visited Birmingham some dozen times from 1840 to 1870, and on most of the early occasions it is believed he stayed at the Old Royal Hotel. On January 6, 1853, Dickens was presented with a silver "Iliad" salver and a diamond ring by the people of Birmingham in grateful acknowledgment of his "varied and well-applied talents." After the presentation the company adjourned to the Old Royal Hotel (then Dee's Hotel), where a banquet took place with the Mayor, Henry Hawkes, in the chair, and Peter Hollins, the sculptor, in the vice-chair.

The company numbered 218, and the event is notable as the occasion on which Dickens made a promise to give, in aid of the Birmingham and Midland Institute, his first public reading from his books.

"It would take about two hours," he said, "with a pause of ten minutes about half-way through. There would be some novelty in the thing, as I have never done it in public, though I have in private, and (if I may say so) with great effect on the hearers."

That was a notable event in Dickens's life, for it is well known what followed from that initial public recital; and the place where the step was taken naturally becomes a landmark in his life; and so the Old Royal Hotel, Birmingham, if for no other reason, claims to be remembered as a notable and important one in Dickens annals.

Chapter XVI

COVENTRY, DUNCHUBCH, AND DAVENTRY INNS, AND THE "SARACEN'S HEAD," TOWCESTER

***

Continuing their journey, the Pickwickians duly reached Coventry. The inn, however, where the post-chaise stopped to change horses is not mentioned by name, but may have been the Castle Hotel there; at any rate, the "Castle" has a Dickensian interest, for it was here that a public dinner was given to Dickens in December, 1858, when he was presented with a gold repeater watch of special construction as a mark of gratitude for his reading of the Christmas Carol, given a year previously in aid of the funds of the Coventry Institute. The hotel was, at the time the Pickwickians arrived there, a posting inn of repute. From Coventry Sam Weller beguiled the time with anecdotes until they reached Dunchurch, "where a dry postboy and fresh horses were procured"; the next stage was Daventry, and in neither case is the name of an inn mentioned or hinted at.

At the end of each stage it rained harder than ever, with the result that when they pulled up at the "Saracen's Head," Towcester, they were in a disconsolate state. Bob Sawyer's apparel, we are told, "shone so with the wet that it might have been mistaken for a full suit of prepared oilskin." In these circumstances, and on the recommendation of the wise Sam, the party decided to stop the night.

"There's beds here, sir," Sam assured his master as a further inducement; "everything clean and comfortable. Very good little dinner, sir, they can get ready in half an hour-pair of fowls, sir, and a weal cutlet; French beans, 'taters, tart and tidiness. You'd better stop vere you are, sir, if I might recommend." At this very moment the host appeared, and, having confirmed Sam's statement, Mr. Pickwick decided to take the "advice" of his trusted servant, which caused the landlord to smile with delight.

The pilgrim to Towcester to-day, searching for the sign of the "Saracen's Head," would find himself on a fruitless errand, for it was changed scores of years back to the Pomfret Arms. Indeed, it was so called at the time The Pickwick Papers were first published, having been altered in 1881 at the bidding of the new lord of the manor when he succeeded to the titles and estates.

But doubtless Dickens knew it in his newspaper reporting days, and described it from memory. In any case, he is historically correct in retaining the old name, for the period of his book is 1827-28. Beyond the change of name the hotel to-day is practically the same as it was in those early days, the only material alteration being the conversion of the kitchen into a bar-parlour and smoking-room, where the open chimney and corner seats have given place to more modern and ornate substitutes.

Situated in the main street this old posting house is a prominent feature. The exterior is typical of the period. It is a low, long-looking building with many windows, two stories high (unless the dormer windows in the old red-tiled roof be counted another), and is built of a light brownish sandstone brick, peculiar to the neighbourhood. There is a picturesque bow window on the ground floor to the left of the solid oak gateway leading into the coach yard, and over this hangs the swinging sign-board flanked on each side by two curious carved figures set in alcoves let into the wall; the whole general setting is a pleasant survival of the old-time days of the coaching era.

There always is an agreeable and comforting relief to the traveller when he at last arrives at the inn at his journey's end, and that feeling will not be dispelled to-day when the old "Saracen's Head" is reached. But to the Pickwickians, on the occasion of their visit, wet to the skin, tired, and sorely out at elbow with the raging element they had just driven through, the "Saracen's Head" must have been a haven of delight indeed; and those few words of instructions from the landlord to make the room ready for them must have been cheerful to their ears, and the result, as described in the following paragraph, a joy to their hearts:

"The candles were brought, the fire was stirred up, and a fresh log of wood thrown on. In ten minutes' time a waiter was laying the cloth for dinner, the curtains were drawn, the fire was blazing brightly, and everything looked (as everything always does in all decent English inns) as if the travellers had been expected and their comforts prepared for days beforehand."

So in this cosy room they gathered, after they had sufficiently dried themselves, and eagerly waited for dinner to be served. To them suddenly reappeared Sam Weller, accompanied by no less a person than the notorious Mr. Pott of the Eatanswill Gazette – who, that worthy had discovered, was also staying in the hotel. He was on his way to the great Buff Ball, to be held at Birmingham the next evening. Needless to say, he was heartily welcomed and an agreement was made to club their dinners. Mr. Pott soon began to entertain the company with gossip about his mission and firebrand intentions, taking the opportunity of letting off some of his best abusive expletives at the expense of his rival paper, the Eatanswill Independent, and its editor.

Incidentally he extolled the genius of one of his staff, and revealed the great secret of how he "crammed" for an article on "Chinese Metaphysics" by turning up the two words in the encyclopaedia and combining his information. He was in the midst of enlivening the proceedings with extracts from his own lucubrations, when his great rival, whom he was abusing, drove up, unknown to him, and booked abed for himself at the same hotel. Mr. Slurk was also making for the great Buff Ball at Birmingham, and, having ordered some refreshment, retired to the kitchen (a custom in those days) to smoke and read in peace.

"Now some demon of discord," writes Dickens, "flying over the 'Saracen's Head' at the moment," prompted Bob Sawyer to suggest to his friends that "it wouldn't be a bad notion to have a cigar by the kitchen fire." They all agreed that it was a good idea, and forth they went – only to find, to their surprise, Mr. Slurk there before them deep in the study of some newspaper. The rival editors both started at each other, and gradually showed symptoms of their ancient rivalry bubbling up, which, by slow but certain process, developed until it eventually precipitated them into a free fight with carpet bag and fire shovel as respective weapons.

The details of this fracas are too well known to need repetition here. Suffice to say that, when the fray was at its height, Mr. Pickwick felt it his duty to intervene, and called upon Sam Weller to part the combatants. This he dexterously did by pulling a meal sack over the head and shoulders of Mr. Pott and thus effectually stopping the conflict. The scene, it will be remembered, was depicted with much spirit by Phiz, the artist who illustrated the book. The rivals parted, peace once more reigned, and the company repaired to their respective beds. In the morning both Mr. Pott and Mr. Slurk were careful to continue their journey in separate coaches before the Pickwickians were stirring, whilst the spectators of the exciting scene went forward to London in their post-chaise a little later.

This incident is one of those that are best remembered in the book, and has made the "Saracen's Head," Towcester, a notable Pickwickian landmark. The old posting inn remains to-day as it was when the book was written, and if the kitchen – as such – is not on view any longer, the same room turned to other uses is there for the faithful disciple to meditate in and visualize the scene for himself; and no doubt he will find that the inn is as famous now for its "French beans, 'taters, tarts and tidiness" as it used to be.

We would, however, suggest to the present owner that the words "formerly the 'Saracen's Head'" should be added to those of the Pomfret Arms Hotel on the sign now hanging so gracefully over the pavement as a guide to the Dickens pilgrim seeking the Pickwickian landmark of the town.

Chapter XVII

"OSBORNE'S," ADELPHI, AND TONY WELLER'S PUBLIC-HOUSE ON SHOOTER'S HILL
***

There is a singular and conspicuous interest attaching to Osborne's Hotel in the Adelphi, for the almost pathetic reason that it was in one of its rooms that Mr. Pickwick first made the momentous announcement of his intention of abandoning his nomadic life of travel and adventure and settling down in "some quiet, pretty neighbourhood in the vicinity of London," where he had taken a house which exactly suited his fancy. And so it may be said that within its four walls the Pickwick Club brought its activities to an end, for on Mr. Pickwick's decision to retire from its ramifications, coupled with the fact that during his absence in the Fleet Prison it had suffered much from internal dissensions, its dissolution was imperative, and to use his own words with which he announced the fact to his friends on the occasion in question, "The Pickwick Club no longer exists."

That was an historic pronouncement, and the room in which it was made naturally becomes a veritable landmark for Pickwickians; and a fitting mark of this distinction might well be made, by the fixing of a tablet on the walls of the historic building, which still stands practically as it was in those adventurous days. The event which first brought Mr. Pickwick and his friends to the hotel was a domestic one; but the occasion did not pass without an awkward adventure such as always dogged the footsteps of the Pickwickians.

Mr. Pickwick had just been released from the Fleet Prison and was at Mr. Perker's office settling little details in connexion with Messrs. Dodson and Fogg, when his old friend Wardle turned up quite unexpectedly to seek the advice of the little lawyer on the situation which had arisen by his daughter Emily's infatuation for Mr. Snodgrass. He had brought his daughter up from Dingley Dell and informed Mr. Pickwick that "she was at Osborne's Hotel in the Adelphi at this moment, unless your enterprising friend has run away with her since I came out this morning."

Mr. Perker made advice unnecessary, for he proved to both of them that they were quite delighted at the prospect. Mr. Wardle forthwith invited them to dine with him, and he sent the fat boy to "Osborne's" with the information that he and Mr. Pickwick would return together at five o'clock. Arriving at the hotel the fat boy went upstairs to execute his commission.

He walked into the sitting-room without previously knocking at the door, and so beheld a gentleman with his arm clasping his young mistress's waist, sitting very lovingly by her side on a sofa, while Arabella and her pretty handmaid feigned to be absorbed in looking out of a window at the other end of the room. At sight of which phenomenon the fat boy uttered an interjection, the ladies a scream, and the gentleman an oath, almost simultaneously.

"Wretched creature, what do you want here?" said the gentleman, who it is needless to say was Mr. Snodgrass.

To this the fat boy, considerably terrified, briefly responded, "Missis."

"What do you want me for?" enquired Emily, turning her head aside, "you stupid creature."

"Master and Mr. Pickwick is a-going to dine here at five," replied the fat boy.

After being bribed by Snodgrass, Emily and Arabella, he was invited by Mary to dine with her downstairs, where he regaled himself on meat pie, steak, a dish of potatoes and a pot of porter. Here he attempted to make love to Mary, and, having failed, "ate a pound or so of steak with a sentimental countenance and fell fast asleep."

"There was so much to say upstairs, and there were so many plans to concert for elopement and matrimony in the event of old Wardle continuing to be cruel, that it wanted only half an hour to dinner when Mr. Snodgrass took his final adieu. The ladies ran to Emily's bedroom to dress, and the lover, taking up his hat, walked out of the room. He had scarcely got outside the door when he heard Wardle's voice talking loudly; and, looking over the banisters, beheld him, followed by some other gentlemen, coming straight upstairs. Knowing nothing of the house, Mr. Snodgrass in his confusion stepped hastily back into the room he had just quitted, and, passing from thence into an inner apartment (Mr. Wardle's bedchamber), closed the door softly, just as the persons he had caught sight of entered the sitting-room. These were Mr. Wardle and Mr. Pickwick, Mr. Nathaniel Winkle and Mr. Benjamin Allen, whom he had no difficulty in recognising by their voices."

In this dilemma Mr. Snodgrass remained, for the door was locked and the key gone, and in desperation he sat himself down upon a portmanteau and trembled violently. In the meantime Mr. Pickwick, Mr. Wardle and the rest of the company settled down to dinner, at which the fat boy made himself conspicuous "by smirking, grinning and winking with redoubled assiduity." His state of mind grew worse, when, having at Mr. Wardle's instructions, gone into the next room to fetch his snuff-box from the dressing-table, he returned with the palest face "that ever a fat boy wore." In his effort to acquaint Mr. Pickwick with what he encountered in the room, his manner became worse and worse, and on the instant that Mr. Wardle was about to ring for the waiters to remove him to a place of safety, Mr. Snodgrass, "the captive lover, his face burning with confusion, suddenly walked in from the bedroom, and made a comprehensive bow to the company."

"Mr. Snodgrass, who had only waited for a hearing, at once recounted how he had been placed in his then distressing predicament; how the fear of giving rise to domestic dissensions had alone prompted him to avoid Mr. Wardle on his entrance; and how he merely meant to depart by another door, but, finding it locked, had been compelled to stay against his will. It was a painful situation to be placed in; but he now regretted it the less, inasmuch as it afforded him an opportunity of acknowledging before their mutual friends that he loved Mr. Wardle's daughter deeply and sincerely, that he was proud to avow that the feeling was mutual, and that if thousands of miles were placed between them, or oceans rolled their waters, he could never for an instant forget those happy days when first – et cetera, et cetera.

"Having delivered himself to this effect Mr. Snodgrass bowed again, looked into the crown of his hat, and stepped towards the door."

But he was stopped on the threshold, and Arabella, having taken up the defence, called on Mr. Wardle to "shake hands with him and order him some dinner." A reconciliation took place and Mr. Snodgrass had dinner at a side-table, and when he had finished drew his chair next to Emily, without the smallest opposition on the old gentleman's part. The remainder of the evening passed off very happily "and all was smiles and shirt collars."

During the next few days much perturbation was evinced by the Pickwickians at their leader's continual absence from the society of his admiring friends, and it being unanimously resolved that he should be called upon to explain himself, Mr. Wardle invited the "full circle" to dinner again at Osborne's Hotel to give him the opportunity. After the decanters "had been twice sent round" Mr. Wardle called upon Mr. Pickwick for his explanation. This was forthcoming in a pathetic speech, very affecting to all present, announcing his unalterable decision of retiring for the rest of his life into the quiet village of Dulwich. "If I have done but little good," he said, by way of peroration, "I trust I have done less harm, and that none of my adventures will be other than a source of amusing and pleasant recollection to me in the decline of life. God bless you all."

With these words Mr. Pickwick filled and drained a bumper with a trembling hand; and his eyes moistened as his friends rose with one accord and pledged him from their hearts. So runs the chronicle, and so ended the immortal Pickwick Club, in the precincts of Osborne's Hotel in the Adelphi, which also became the headquarters of the relatives of Mr. Wardle during their stay in London for the wedding of his daughter. From here the wedding party set out for Mr. Pickwick's new abode at Dulwich, from which house the ceremony took place, and where the wedding was celebrated by a happy breakfast party afterwards.

To have the distinction of being the venue for such notable events is something that any self-respecting hotel should be proud of, and we are sure that Osborne's Hotel will be remembered so long as it stands for those reasons alone. But it has other reasons for fame, even if they are more likely to be forgotten, or lightly passed over by those who keep the records of London's notable landmarks. It stands to-day in a neighbourhood distinguished for its history, and has claims to a share in the making of that history.

It is situated, as it has always been, at the corner of John and Adam Streets, and was first opened in 1777 as the Adelphi New Tavern and Coffee House. Dickens no doubt knew it well, for the Adelphi and its neighbourhood attracted him greatly, and its curious old buildings, side streets and rambling arches often figure in his books. When a mere boy at work in the blacking factory, down by the river there, he continually wandered about its quaint byways. "Osborne's" was a notable house in those days, and if its full records were available, no doubt many an entertaining story concerning its activities could be told. As it is, it is known that "being completely fitted up in the most elegant and convenient manner for the entertainment of noblemen and gentlemen," as it boasted in its early days, many notable figures in past history made it their headquarters.

On the 8th August, 1787, Gibbon stayed there on his arrival from Lausanne with the completion of his "History," and wrote to Lord Sheffield to apprise him of the fact. In 1802 Isaac D'Israeli, the author of Curiosities of Literature and father of the famous Earl of Beaconsfield, stayed in the hotel after his honeymoon. It is also on record that George Crabbe, the poet, with his wife resided for a time there, and that Rowlandson, the caricaturist, died in one of its rooms in 1827.

Perhaps the most notorious of visitors to it were the King and Queen of the Sandwich Islands in 1824. Unfortunately, both were victims to the smallpox epidemic which raged at the time, and died in the hotel, the latter on the 8th July of that year and the former on the 14th September. The visit of the "illustrious" king, we are told, gave rise to the popular song, "The King of the Cannibal Islands."

During the war it was acquired as a house of utility for the military. Before it was acquired for that purpose it was the favoured resort of business men of the neighbourhood and of certain literary and artistic coteries, and was the headquarters of the famous O.P. Club. However, it has returned now to its old-time ways and methods, and we hope it will long remain a landmark for the Dickens lover and particularly the Pickwickian devotee.

The last tavern mentioned in The Pickwick Papers is the "excellent public-house near Shooter's Hill," to which Mr. Weller, senior, retired. Unfortunately it was never named, nor has it been identified. Continuing to drive a coach for twelve months after the Pickwick Club had ceased to exist, he became afflicted with gout and was compelled to give up his lifelong calling. The contents of his pocket-book had been so well invested by Mr. Pickwick, we are told, that he had a handsome independence for the purpose of his last days. At Shooter's Hill he was quite reverenced as an oracle, boasting very much of his intimacy with Mr. Pickwick, and retaining a most unconquerable aversion to widows.

Chapter XVIII

PICKWICK AND THE "GEORGE" INN
***

Certain traditional legends naturally grow round our old London landmarks and, when once started, no matter how conjectural, they are hard to overtake or suppress.

The George Inn, Southwark, is an instance of this, and the legend that is prone to cling to it is that it was the original of the White Hart Inn of Pickwick fame; the contention being that Dickens, when writing so faithfully of the "White Hart" in Chapter X of The Pickwick Papers, where Sam Weller was first discovered, described the "George" and called it after its near neighbour, the "White Hart." This contention, we submit, has no justification whatever. The only reason, therefore, for referring to it here, is with a view to dispelling the illusion.

It is surprising that so good a Dickensian as the late J. Ashby Sterry should have been one of those who favoured the idea. Whether he was the first to do so we are not aware. But in his very interesting and informative article entitled "Dickens in Southwark," in The English Illustrated Magazine for November, 1888, he states it as his opinion that the "George" was the original of the "White Hart," and reverted to the same idea in The Bystander (1901). The following extract from the former article contains the argument he used to substantiate his claim:

"Moreover it (the 'George') is especially notable as being the spot where Mr. Pickwick first encountered the immortal Sam Weller. The 'White Hart' is the name, I am aware, given in the book, but it is said that Dickens changed the sign in order that the place should not be too closely identified. This was by no means an unusual custom with the novelist. I think he did the same thing in Edwin Drood, where the 'Bull' at Rochester is described under the sign of the 'Blue Boar.' A similar change was made in Great Expectations, where the same inn is disguised in like fashion, in the account of the dinner given after Pip was bound apprentice to Joe Gargery. The 'White Hart' is close by, on the same side of the way, a little nearer London Bridge, but little, if anything, is remaining of the old inn, and the whole of the place and its surroundings have been modernised.

"I, however, had the opportunity of comparing both inns some years ago, and have no hesitation in saying that the 'George' is the inn where the irrepressible Alfred Jingle and the elderly Miss Rachel were discovered by the warm-hearted, hot-tempered Wardle. If you like to go upstairs you can see the very room where Mr. Jingle consented to forfeit all claims to the lady's hand for the consideration of a hundred and twenty pounds. Cannot you fancy, too, the landlord shouting instructions from those picturesque flower-decked galleries to Sam in the yard below?"

These deductions and views are not in any way convincing to us; indeed, we find ourselves in complete disagreement with them, and few Dickensians, we feel sure, will endorse them.

Mr. Ashby Sterry's argument regarding the "Bull" and the "Blue Boar" at Rochester proves nothing. Dickens described the "Bull" there in The Pickwick Papers and called it the "Bull" at Rochester, as he did the "Leather Bottle" at Cobham, the "Angel" at Bury St. Edmunds, the "Great White Horse" at Ipswich – to name a few parallel cases. When he described the "Bull" and called it the "Blue Boar," it was in another book, Great Expectations, not in Edwin Drood, as stated by Mr. Ashby Sterry, and its location was a fictitious city, i.e. The Market Town.

The only case in which Dickens deliberately used the name of one inn for another was that of the "Maypole" and "King's Head" at Chigwell in Barnaby Rudge. But in this instance he admitted that he had done so, although it was scarcely necessary, for the inns were very dissimilar and the novelist's description of the latter could not be taken for the former.

The case of the "George" and the "White Hart" is different. They both stood quite near to each other at the time Dickens was writing The Pickwick Papers, and were both so named and both famous. There could be no reason, therefore, for him to describe one and call it by the other's name.

Although they may not have been identical in all particulars as to structure, the "George" and the "White Hart" were sufficiently alike to make it possible for a person of imagination to go over the "George" and be satisfied that such and such a room might do for the one in which "Mr. Jingle forfeited all claims to the lady's hand," and imagine, too, that the galleries could be accepted easily as those over which "the landlord shouted instructions to Sam in the Yard." But these flights of fancy could be indulged in even n the New Inn, Gloucester, or any similar old coaching inn, if one so desired.

Mr. Percy FitzGerald, the greatest authority on The Pickwick Papers, is of the same opinion as ourselves on the point, and asks: "Why should notoriety be attached to the 'White Hart,' from which the 'George' was to be shielded?"

No, the "George" is a wonderfully alluring old inn, and for this reason Dickensians have a warm place in their hearts for it. But we have no hesitation in saying that it is not the original of the "White Hart" of Pickwick and Sam Weller fame.

Another distinguished writer, the American novelist and artist, F. Hopkinson Smith, in his book, Dickens's London, fell into a similar blunder. Indeed, his book contains some glaring mistakes, owing, no doubt, to the fact, which he admits, that he gathered his information from any Tom, Dick or Harry he came in contact with during his wanderings. In describing his visit to the "George," he found incidents from Pickwick to fit every nook and cranny in the building and quoted them with much conviction. But he quoted no facts, nor did he give any data to substantiate his statements. Someone told him it was the original of the "White Hart," as they told him that the house named Dickens House in Lant Street was where Dickens once lived, irrespective of the fact that the actual house was demolished years before. Yet that satisfied him, he took no trouble to make further enquiries and then imagined the rest. In regard to the "George" he let his imagination run riot, dilated on this being Miss Wardle's room, this being the room where the couple were discovered, and further states that Dickens made the inn a favourite one of his when a boy in Lant Street, and speaks of the seat he used to sit in. All of which is sheer nonsense.

Dickens may have known the George Inn in those early days, but being only a mere boy is not likely to have frequented it. Although in later years – those of Little Dorrit and the Uncommercial Traveller – it is quite likely he may have visited it. Indeed, Miss Murray, the present hostess, tells us he did. Her authority was Abraham Dawson, a well-known carman and carrier in days gone by, who was a nephew of W. S. Scholefield who owned the inn at the time. Dawson assured her that he frequently chatted with Dickens in the coffee-room.

Yet the only occasion, so far as we are aware, that the novelist actually mentions the inn is in Little Dorrit, Book I, Chapter XXII, where Maggy, speaking of Tip, says: "If he goes into the 'George' and writes a letter..."

No, the George Inn is just a fine survival of old days – the old days of which Dickens wrote – and is similar, in many respects, to what the 'White Hart' used to be. As such Dickensians have a great affection for it, and there is no need to invent stories about it to justify their reverence.

Mr. A. St. John Adcock is another writer who steers clear of the confusion. In The Booklover's London, after referring to the "White Hart," he goes on to say: "If you step aside up George Yard, which is next to the 'White Hart' yard, you may see the old George

Inn which, with its low ceilings, ancient rafters and old wooden galleries outside, closely resembles what the 'White Hart' used to be, and gives us an idea of the inn yards in which the strolling players of Shakespeare's time used to set up their stages."

Let us leave it at that and retain our regard for the old inn for what it is, rather than for what it is not.

www.ReadHowYouWant.com

You can buy our **Large Type** and **EasyRead** books from our www.ReadHowYouWant.com website, from websites like Amazon.com and through your UK and North American bookshop.

EasyRead books are designed to make your reading easy and enjoyable. **EasyRead** books are published in different font sizes, so you can select the font size best for you.

EasyRead is for people with normal eyesight who want books in an easy-to-read format.

EasyRead Comfort is for people who find reading small print tiring but do not need large print.

EasyRead Large is for people who find it easier to read larger print.

EasyRead Large Bold is for people with retinal problems who need to read high contrast text.

EasyRead Super Large is for people who require large and dense format, available in 18pt, 20pt and 24pt.

The **EasyRead** font, character, word and line spacing have all been set to make it as easy as possible both to recognize a word, and to run your eye along a line of text without losing your place. We split as few words as possible at line ends, as split words make reading harder and can be annoying. For out-of-copyright books, words have been changed to modern spelling (where the sense is not affected), and the original hyphenation of compound words has been retained where this improves word recognition or sense.

With most things you buy, you get a choice, and you can choose the make and model that suits best. There is a big exception – books. You don't get to choose a format that is easy for you to read – you have to read the format the publisher selects.

This **"One Size Fits All"** paradigm **no longer** need apply to books.

At www.ReadHowYouWant.com, you can order a book just as you want it, so you can read it easily. You can choose nearly any format, and at a surprisingly low cost, because of a technical breakthrough that allows us to typeset an individual book automatically, print and bind the book and have it quickly sent directly to you.

You can have your book in **Talking Book** formats (**DAISY or MP3**) or as an **E-book** or in **Braille**.

We have developed totally new visual formats which we hope will help people with **dyslexia** and other print reading disabilities. Look at www.ReadHowYouWant.com for more information.

Good news for publishers and authors. There is a big market for large type, personalized and accessible format books. We can help publishers and authors find new market opportunities for their books, and selling your book through www.ReadHowYouWant.com is easy – we do the work for you. Contact us on info@ReadHowYouWant.com.

Made in the USA
Columbia, SC
29 December 2024